INTERACTIONS

a poetry teaching anthology

compiled and edited by Geoffrey Halson

Longman

LONGMAN GROUP LIMITED
Longman House
Burnt Mill, Harlow, Essex CM20 2JE, England

First published 1982
ISBN 0 582 33127 7

Set in 11/12 Linotron 202 Baskerville

Printed in Singapore
by Singapore National Printers (Pte) Ltd

Contents

Introduction

One of the aims of this anthology is to illustrate the wide-ranging concern of poets, whether they are major literary figures or the anonymous writers of broadsheet verses, with the experiences of everyday living. 'The objects of the Poet's thoughts are everywhere,' wrote Wordsworth. That this is so is evident in this collection. Many of the poems here are concerned with personal feelings, about the private side of one's life – being in love, relating to one's parents, having children, getting old, for instance. Many are concerned with the relationship of the individual to the society in which he lives and with the attitudes of society towards the individual. The range of 'the objects of the poet's thoughts' may well surprise; we readily accept that novelists and dramatists should write of life in all its aspects but we still tend to regard the poet as existing in a state remote from life. Yet, here, we can find Wordsworth condemning the railway planners of the 1840s as Betjeman later condemns the town and country planners of our own times; Thom Gunn analysing the motivations of young motorcyclists; Leslie Norris identifying with the problems of a Welsh rural community facing eviction so that a valley can be flooded to make a reservoir; an anonymous broadsheet poet celebrating a literally 'hot' piece of local news – the burning down of Liverpool's floating landing stage in 1874.

Although one of the advantages of an anthology is the freedom it gives for the reader to select and sample, this freedom can have disadvantages where no guidelines exist. *Interactions* seeks to supply several guidelines. It is essentially a shaped anthology and the accompanying notes have been designed to reflect this. It can be read, and studied, as a continuous sequence in which successive themes develop one from another. Within this continuous sequence the poems have been arranged in groups so that comparisons can be made between poems dealing with similar or contrasting aspects of a particular subject. A complete reference guide to the sequence of subjects can be found in the headlines introducing each group of poems in the Contents on pages 3 to 8.

How these continuous sequences are arranged can be illustrated by turning to Elizabeth Jennings's 'Old Woman' (p. 58), the final poem in the group headed *Views from old age*. It is partly concerned with the reactions of an elderly woman towards some of her possessions. The next group of poems, *Possessions* (p. 61), presents a sequence of contrasting views of domestic possessions after their original owners have died. In the next group, *Moving on*, Heather Buck's contemporary poem 'Moving House (p. 66) and William Barnes's nineteenth-century dialect poem 'Leady-Day an' Ridden House' (p. 67) are concerned not only with possessions but also with the major upheaval of moving house; whilst the final poem in the group, 'Glenaradale' (p. 69) considers not only the upheaval of moving house but also the tragedy of being dispossessed of one's home in the nineteenth century in order to clear part of the Scottish Highlands for the development of vast shooting estates for aristocratic landlords and their friends. 'Glenaradale' raises issues involving *national* feelings and these feelings are developed in the four groups of poems (*National views*) which follow.

Much can be missed in a poem when it is read and studied without reference to the circumstances in which it was written. A poem is often highly sensitive to the spirit of the age in which it was written, and it may also be responsive to group influences – as in the case of the so-called 'Georgian poets' or the poetry of 'the Auden circle'. Poetry can often be more readily enjoyed, appreciated and identified with if one knows something of its background. For this reason brief comments about the poet, the social or historical background of the poem, and the people or events referred to in the poem have been included, where relevant, in the editorial notes at the end of each group of poems. As well as providing relevant information they aim to help the reader to explore the poems. The questions are included solely to encourage discussion; they are meant to provide ideas and thoughts rather than definitive interpretations.

The title of this anthology, *Interactions*, provides a one-word summary of its scope and of the processes involved in the writing, reading and study of poetry. The interaction between the poet and 'the objects of the poet's thoughts' inspires the poem. When we read a poem there is interaction between the poet's view of his or her subject and our response to that view. If we look at a group of poems which reveal the responses of a number of poets to the same general theme, the poems within the group interact when read and studied. Finally, the fullest interpretation of the meaning of a poem can often be achieved through the interacting thoughts of a number of readers discussing the poem. This last process of interaction is one which can make classroom discussion of poetry the most rewarding, stimulating and exciting area of literary study. This discussion can produce an extending of human experience which poetry, the most private and personal form of literary expression, is very apt to provide.

Geoffrey Halson

Reservoir Street

In nineteen twenty-six, the year
Of the Strike, on a day of bubbling heat
I went to stay with my sun-faced cousins
Who lived in a house on Reservoir Street.

Auntie stood strong as the Eddystone Lighthouse.
A terrible light shone out of her head.
Her children scuttled like ships for harbour.
You must let them know what's what, she said.

Her five prime-beef boys circled round me.
They didn't enjoy what they saw at all.
We couldn't make any more of each other
Than the map of stains on the bedroom wall.

All night long on the road to the city
The motor-car tyres rubbed out the dark.
Early in the morning I watched from the window
The sun like a killer come out of the park.

Down in the reservoir I saw a man drowning.
His flooding head came over the side.
They poked him out of a parcel of water.
He's poisoned the drink! my cousins cried.

I packed my bag and I said to Auntie,
I think I'll go home on the one o'clock train.
My, they all said, he wants his mammy.
They never let me forget it again.

Through the Cornish jungle-country
Like a parrot the train screamed home.
I thought of my brother who slept beside me,
Four walls round us pure as cloam![1]

When I got to the house my head was thunder.
The bed lay open as a shell.
Sweet was my brother's kiss, and sweeter
The innocent water from the well.

Charles Causley

[1] clay

Norfolk

How did the Devil come? When first attack?
    These Norfolk lanes recall lost innocence,
The years fall off and find me walking back
    Dragging a stick along the wooden fence
Down this same path where, forty years ago,
My father strolled behind me, calm and slow.

I used to fill my hand with sorrel seeds
    And shower him with them from the tops of stiles,
I used to butt my head into his tweeds
    To make him hurry down those languorous miles
Of ash and alder-shaded lanes, till here
Our moorings and the masthead would appear.

There after supper lit by lantern light
    Warm in the cabin I could lie secure
And hear against the polished sides at night
    The lap lap lapping of the weedy Bure,
A whispering and watery Norfolk sound
Telling of all the moonlit reeds around.

How did the Devil come? When first attack?
    The church is just the same, though now I know
Fowler of Louth restored[1] it. Time, bring back
    The rapturous ignorance of long ago,
The peace before the dreadful daylight starts,
Of unkept promises and broken hearts.

John Betjeman

[1] In the nineteenth century it became fashionable to 'restore' churches – i.e. to repair and alter them in order to bring them back as nearly as possible to their original form. Many of these 'restorations' are now regarded by enthusiasts for old churches (John Betjeman amongst them) as being in very doubtful taste and as having destroyed the character of many churches.

NOTES

Reservoir Street

Charles Causley admits to being 'obsessed by the theme of lost innocence' and this is one of a number of poems about childhood which he has written using the simple verse form of the old ballads. The simplicity of the verse form helps the reader to enter quickly into the child's world whilst at the same time the stark economy of expression demands that the implications of every detail and every image need careful consideration. In 'Reservoir Street' the experience of seeing the man being fished out of the reservoir is made the more dreadful for the boy because of his inability to communicate with his cousins and because of the way in which his aunt and her five sons possess such intimidating physical presence.

How are the boy's impressions of the visit and the events of the visit conveyed by specific details and images? (Consider the Eddystone Lighthouse image, for instance, and the references to 'sun-faced cousins' and 'prime-beef boys'.) In what ways is the insensitivity of the boy's cousins and, maybe, his aunt, revealed in the poem? What are the implications of the statement 'the bed lay open as a shell' and of the description of the well water as 'innocent' in the last verse?

Norfolk

The prompting to write is often at its most powerful when one revisits places associated with idyllically happy or with intensely sad events in one's past. Here, a return visit to Norfolk by John Betjeman creates memories, easily and intensely conveyed to paper, of a childhood holiday there.

Look carefully at the memories John Betjeman chooses to recall. What is significant about the selection in terms of the impressions he is intent on conveying and of his motives for recalling his memories?

Like 'Reservoir Street', 'Norfolk' is concerned with lost innocence, but with John Betjeman there is the suggestion that lost innocence is not something associated exclusively with human failings such as 'unkept promises and broken hearts'. Notice that he twice asks: 'How did the Devil come? When first attack?'. Is he drawing a parallel between the 'rapturous ignorance' of his childhood and the rapturous ignorance of Adam and Eve in the Garden of Eden before they were tempted by the Devil into partaking of the Tree of Knowledge? Does the 'dreadful daylight' start with the dawn of knowledge in the child?

Dylan Thomas's great poem 'Fern Hill' also draws parallels between the rapture of childhood and the rapture of Adam and Eve – 'So it must have been after the birth of the simple light in the first, spinning place...'

Looking On

Hearing our voices raised –
Perhaps in anger,
Or in some trivial argument
That is not anger –
She screams until we stop,
And smile, and look at her,
Poised on the sheer drop
Which opens under her.

If these, her parents, show
How the gods can fail,
Squabbling on Olympus,
How can she fail
To see that anarchy
Is what one must expect,
That to be happy
One must be circumspect?

But the reverse is true
Also, when we kiss
Seeing herself excluded
Even from that kiss.
The gods' too gross affairs
Make myths for innocent men,
So the innocent eye stares
At love in its den.

Like a strange motley beast
Out of an old myth,
Anger and love together
Make up her own myth,
Of these two who cherish,
Protect, feed, deny,
In whose arms she will flourish
Or else will die.

Anthony Thwaite

Bye Baby Bunting

The little girl is dancing in the front room
her feet are faster than fear
her voice is louder than the television

she will not hear her father
who is leaving
who is closing the back door as quietly as he can
who has left a huge rocking horse wrapped in guilt

The girl dances up and down the cold corridor
she is on points
her arms stretch

Her father is sending her postcards
from different places
he is everywhere and nowhere
there is no address

The girl rocks higher than her rocking horse
she will not listen to her mother
who is talking about money
who is letting the front room
who has placed a new chain on the back door

The girl spins like a globe of the world
she is everywhere and nowhere
her outline blurs

Valerie Sinason

NOTES

Looking On

Sometimes the title of a poem is an integral part of the whole experience of the poem. What are the disturbing implications of this title? Just as John Betjeman adds a provocative dimension to 'Norfolk' (p. 12) by his reference to the Devil, so Anthony Thwaite here emphasises the fundamental primitive dilemmas of the relationships between father and mother, and between parents and child, by referring to Greek mythology. What do his refer-

16

ences to mythology tell you about the parallels between man's original need for a mythology to bring order and security to his life and the child's need for a mythology built around her parents which will bring order and security to her life? What would appear to be the purpose of 'a strange motley beast' in man's early myths? In what ways is the concept of the child's innocence similar to or different from the concept presented in John Betjeman's 'Norfolk'?

Anthony Thwaite suggests that both anger and love possess the power to exclude a child from its parents. Do you agree? (For an interesting look at a parent's feelings of exclusion from his child see David Holbrook's poem 'Fingers in the Door' where, in seeking in vain to comfort his child after he had accidentally closed her fingers in a door, he feels suddenly 'light-years from any mutual help or comfort'.)

A further consideration of man's primitive need to establish a sense of order through mythology can be found in Patric Dickinson's poem 'Jodrell Bank' on page 114 of this anthology.

Bye Baby Bunting

What are the implications of this title? (Bear in mind the second line of the old rhyme.)

This is a good example of a poem in which its meaning is enlarged by its mode of construction. What effects of the father's departure on the little girl are suggested by the absence of punctuation, by the accumulation of statements commencing with 'who', by the frequent use of continuous tenses ('is leaving' ... 'is closing'), by the use of comparative forms of adjectives ('faster', 'higher'), by the repetition of 'everywhere and nowhere', and by the overall sense of continuous movement?

How does the poem perhaps give strength to Anthony Thwaite's contentions in 'Looking On' and provide an illustration of the 'sheer drop' which a child instinctively fears?

It is interesting to note that Valerie Sinason has done a considerable amount of work with troubled children and has trained in child psychotherapy.

Snaring and Birds-nesting

Well I call to mind
('Twas at an early age, ere I had seen
Nine summers) when upon the mountain slope
The frost, and breath of frosty wind, had snapped
The last autumnal crocus, 'twas my joy
To wander half the night among the cliffs
And the smooth hollows where the woodcocks ran
Along the open turf. In thought and wish
That time, my shoulder all with springes[1] hung,
I was a fell destroyer. On the heights
Scudding away from snare to snare, I plied
My anxious visitation, hurrying on,
Still hurrying, hurrying onward; – moon and stars
Were shining o'er my head. I was alone,
And seemed to be a trouble to the peace
That was among them. Sometimes it befell
In these night wanderings, that a strong desire
O'erpowered my better reason, and the bird
Which was the captive of another's toils
Became my prey; and when the deed was done
I heard among the solitary hills
Low breathings coming after me, and sounds
Of undistinguishable motion, steps
Almost as silent as the turf they trod.

      Nor less in springtime when on southern banks
The shining sun had from his knot of leaves
Decoyed the primrose flower, and when the Vales
And woods were warm, was I a plunderer then
In the high places, on the lonesome peaks
Where'er, among the mountains and the winds,
The mother-bird had built her lodge; though mean
My object and inglorious, yet the end
Was not ignoble. Oh! when I have hung
Above the raven's nest, by knots of grass
And half-inch fissures in the slippery rock
But ill sustained, and almost (as it seemed)
Suspended by the blast which blew amain,
Shouldering the naked crag, oh, at that time
While on the perilous ridge I hung alone,
With what strange utterance did the loud dry wind

[1] snares for catching small game, especially birds.

Blow through my ears! the sky seemed not a sky
Of earth – and with what motion moved the clouds!

William Wordsworth

(from Book 1, 'Childhood and School-time', of *The Prelude*
in its original version of 1805)

'Busy meddling joys'

The cow-boy still cuts short the day,
By mingling mischief with his play;
Oft in the pond, with weeds o'ergrown,
Hurling quick the plashing stone
To cheat his dog, who watching lies,
And instant plunges for the prize;
And though each effort proves in vain,
He shakes his coat, and dives again,
Till, wearied with the fruitless play,
He drops his tail, and sneaks away,
Nor longer heeds the bawling boy,
Who seeks new sports with added joy:
Now on some bank's o'er hanging brow
Beating the wasp's nest with a bough,
Till armies from the hole appear,
And threaten vengeance in his ear
With such determined hue-and-cry
As makes the bold besieger fly;
Then, pelting with excessive glee
The squirrel on the woodland-tree,
Who nimbles round from grain to grain,
And cocks his tail, and peeps again,
Half pleased, as if he thought the fray
Which mischief made was meant for play,
Till scared and startled into flight,
He instant tumbles out of sight.
Thus he his leisure hour employs,
And feeds on busy meddling joys,
While in the willow-shaded pool
His cattle stand, their hides to cool.

John Clare

(from 'July' in *The Shepherd's Calendar*)

NOTES

Snaring and Birds-nesting

The early sections of Wordsworth's long autobiographical and philosophical poem *The Prelude* are concerned with experiences of his childhood and youth in The Lake District in the 1770s and 1780s. The events referred to in this passage took place during Wordsworth's first year at Hawkshead Grammar School.

What aspects of the experiences described are typical of an ordinary country boy's enjoyment of solitary expeditions and what aspects suggest that the young Wordsworth was especially sensitive to the atmosphere of his outdoor surroundings? How does Wordsworth convey the intensity of these childhood experiences to his readers?

'Busy meddling joys'

John Clare's sequence of poems entitled *The Shepherd's Calendar* was published in 1827. The poems present an authentic and highly atmospheric view of the country life and landscapes around Clare's home area on the edge of the Fen country a few miles to the north of Peterborough. Clare was of a humbler origin than Wordsworth, and this is reflected in his exactly observed descriptions of shepherds, hedgers, weeders, woodmen, threshers, mowers and other country labourers. During his early youth Clare himself worked as a bird-scarer, a horse-boy and a plough-boy.

The cow-boy of this passage would have been little more than a child. How does Clare convey the cow-boy's childish mischievousness and how does he reveal his appreciation not only of the motivations of the boy but also of the instinctive reactions of the dog, the wasps and the squirrel? What gives the passage its sense of busy movement? In what ways does the passage convey the impression of being written by an observant countryman who has witnessed such scenes at first hand and who readily identifies with them?

In what ways do you find the descriptions of country life different in these two passages by Wordsworth and Clare? What seem to be the contrasting intentions of Wordsworth and Clare in presenting these descriptions, and how are these contrasting intentions reflected in the style and language of each passage? Why is Clare's use of rhyming couplets and Wordsworth's use of blank verse apt in each case?

First Love

That was her beginning, an apparition
of rose in the unbreathed airs of his love,
her heart revealed by the wash of summer
sprung from her childhood's shallow stream.

Then it was that she put up her hair,
inscribed her eyes with a look of grief,
while her limbs grew as curious as coral branches,
her breast full of secrets.

But the boy, confused in his day's desire,
was searching for herons, his fingers bathed
in the green of walnuts, or watching at night
the Great Bear spin from the maypole star.

It was then that he paused in the death of a game,
felt the hook of her hair on his swimming throat,
saw her mouth at large in the dark river
flushed like a salmon.

But he covered his face and hid his joy
in a wild-goose web of false directions,
and hunted the woods for eggs and glow-worms,
for rabbits tasteless as moss.

And she walked in fields where the crocuses
branded her feet, where mares' tails sprang
from the prancing lake, and the salty grasses
surged round her stranded body.

Laurie Lee

A Frosty Night

'Alice, dear, what ails you,
        Dazed and lost and shaken?
Has the chill night numbed you?
        Is it fright you have taken?'

'Mother, I am very well,
        I was never better.
Mother, do not hold me so,
        Let me write my letter.'

'Sweet, my dear, what ails you?'
        'No, but I am well.
The night was cold and frosty –
        There's no more to tell.'

'Ay, the night was frosty,
        Coldly gaped the moon,
Yet the birds seemed twittering
        Through green boughs of June.

'Soft and thick the snow lay,
        Stars danced in the sky –
Not all the lambs of May-day
        Skip so bold and high.

'Your feet were dancing, Alice,
        Seemed to dance on air,
You looked a ghost or angel
        In the star-light there.

'Your eyes were frosted star-light;
        Your heart, fire and snow,
Who was it said, "I love you"?'
        'Mother, let me go!'

Robert Graves

NOTES

First Love

The feminine awareness and confidence and the masculine awareness and hesitancy, the delicate and fragile nature of first love –
these qualities are explored in this most sensitive and subtly detailed poem. In this type of poem one is too easily tempted into a
state of being beguiled by its beautiful sounds and thus into
underestimating the implications of very deliberately conceived
phrases and images. One can only indicate a few provocative
areas for thought here. For instance, what is implied by the very
positive opening statement, 'That was her beginning' and by the
word 'beginning' in particular? Does the use of the word 'inscribed' in the second verse suggest any special degree of deliberation in the girl's behaviour? What suggestions are there, in the
third and fourth verses, of the oblique ways in which a boy's love
is manifested? Consider, for instance, the way he looks at and,
perhaps unconsciously, interprets objects seemingly unconnected
with the girl. What confusion of feeling is indicated in 'a wild-
goose web of false directions'? How does one interpret the image
of the girl's 'stranded body'?

A Frosty Night

After Laurie Lee's exploration of first love as experienced by a boy
and a girl, Robert Graves's poem focuses on that potentially
traumatic event in family life when the closed circle of family love
is broken by a son's or daughter's 'first love'.

How is the dramatic impact of this poem heightened by
Robert Graves's use of the terse question and response style of the
old ballads such as 'Lord Randal' or 'Edward'? What is the effect
of his also using examples of poetic diction and sentence inver-
sion? Do these stylistic effects detract from the reality of the situation described or do they rather emphasise the solemnity of the
event for the mother?

Underneath the formal structure of the poem how typical do
you find the attitudes taken by mother and daughter to each
other? What symbolic significance emerges from the seasonal imagery used to contrast the frosty conditions with the vitality of the
daughter? What, in view of this use of seasonal images, are the
implications of the poem's title? To whom does Robert Graves
appear most sensitive and sympathetic here, and why?

On the Move

'Man, you gotta Go'

The blue jay scuffling in the bushes follows
Some hidden purpose, and the gust of birds
That spurts across the field, the wheeling swallows,
Have nested in the trees and undergrowth.
Seeking their instinct, or their poise, or both,
One moves with an uncertain violence
Under the dust thrown by a baffled sense
Or the dull thunder of approximate words.

On motorcycles, up the road, they come:
Small, black, as flies hanging in the heat, the Boys,
Until the distance throws them forth, their hum
Bulges to thunder held by calf and thigh.
In goggles, donned impersonality,
In gleaming jackets trophied with the dust,
They strap in doubt – by hiding it, robust –
And almost hear a meaning in their noise.

Exact conclusion of their hardiness
Has no shape yet, but from known whereabouts
They ride, direction where the tires press.
They scare a flight of birds across the field:
Much that is natural, to the will must yield.
Men manufacture both machine and soul,
And use what they imperfectly control
To dare a future from the taken routes.

It is a part solution, after all.
One is not necessarily discord
On earth; or damned because, half animal,
One lacks direct instinct, because one wakes
Afloat on movement that divides and breaks.
One joins the movement in a valueless world,
Choosing it, till, both hurler and the hurled,
One moves as well, always toward, toward.

A minute holds them, who have come to go:
The self-defined, astride the created will
They burst away; the towns they travel through
Are home for neither bird nor holiness,

For birds and saints complete their purposes.
At worst, one is in motion; and at best,
Reaching no absolute, in which to rest,
One is always nearer by not keeping still.

Thom Gunn, California

Provincial Undergraduate

The draggled hair, stained sweater, rumpled slacks,
Eyes staring angrily out of a young face,
Hand nervously dabbing a cigarette
Out against a wall as though it was somebody's face.
He grunts, not argues, grins rather than laughs when
Somebody's tried to do something and failed again.

That somebody! How he hates him! Whoever he is –
From a better school, maybe, or dressed up to kill,
Who can grow a beard, throw parties, pay out cash,
Who can always get the prettiest girls at will.
He covertly kicks his ankles in a queue,
Or lounges across his path. What else can he do?

'After puberty, only the glands want to learn'
Says Goole who weighs up students at a sneer
And finds them wanting. Wanting to get out and earn,
Wanting to be loved, respected, – maybe, feared.
A place in the world? A good job? Goole, you
Failed to teach him what else there was to do.

What else *is* there? He's got to get a degree
Somehow, writes essays on half-known facts.
They're ticked, gone over, somehow rejected. He
Must do better next time, re-read, re-think, go back –
Go back in anger, resign, though not resigned,
Looking for what he does not want to find.

Philip Hobsbaum

25

NOTES

On the Move

Thom Gunn has lived in the United States for a long time and this poem was written there. It reveals his interest in the psychological motivations of young men who take up motorcycling and who wear the gear associated with it as part of a protest cult. Thom Gunn has claimed that this interest was influenced by films such as *The Wild Ones* (one of the earliest post-war American films exploring the violent world of teenage motor-cycle gangs and starring Marlon Brando) and *Rebel without a Cause* (a film starring James Dean, who became a cult figure overnight after dying in a road crash more violent than anything associated with his rebellious screen roles).

What is Thom Gunn keen to establish in the opening lines of the first verse in terms of the contrast between the motivations of bird movements and the motivations of human movements? Note words such as 'hidden purpose', 'instinct' and 'poise' contrasting with 'uncertain violence', 'baffled sense', 'approximate words'. (This contrast in motivation between birds and humans is also explored in Ted Hughes's poem 'Thrushes'.)

In the second verse the contradictions between the superficial cocksureness of the motorcyclists and their underlying lack of purpose and confidence emerge. Examine the meanings of phrases such as 'donned impersonality', 'trophied with the dust' (why use the word 'trophied'?) and statements such as 'They strap in doubt' and 'almost hear a meaning in their noise'.

If, in the third verse, one compares the motorcyclists riding in a 'direction where the tires press' with the actions of the birds in the first verse, what is suggested about the motivations of the motorcyclists? What significance does Thom Gunn give to their scaring of the flight of birds? (Look carefully at the line which follows.) Do the last three lines in any way link the albeit unproductive actions of the motorcyclists with uses of man's willpower which, in other circumstances, *are* productive? (The word 'dare' seems to suggest such a link.)

How, in the fourth verse, does Thom Gunn link the movement of the motorcyclists with the fundamental disadvantage of man on earth – the possession of intellect which overrules the operation of 'direct instinct' and thus makes him '*half* animal'? How do the motorcyclists in their way represent a response to 'a valueless world'? What double implications exist in the use of the word 'movement' here?

In the final verse what unconscious significance does the motorcycle have for its rider? (Note 'astride the created will' in this verse, 'Much that is natural, to the will must yield' in verse 3, and the 'thunder held by calf and thigh' in verse 2.) What is the purpose of the reference to 'birds and saints'? What is Thom Gunn's ultimate justification for the motorcyclists' travelling? What thus become the implications of the poem's title and sub-title? How do 'the Boys' reflect the society in which they live?

Thom Gunn's poems 'Black Jackets' and 'Elvis Presley' would make interesting follow-up reading here.

Provincial Undergraduate

Are there any parallels, do you think, between the attitudes of the motorcyclist who 'joins the movement in a valueless world' in Thom Gunn's poem and the attitudes of the 'Provincial Under-graduate' in this poem? To what extent does the word 'provincial' in the title represent a possible source of this undergraduate's animosity? Is the animosity in part activated by feelings of social inferiority? What is Philip Hobsbaum's purpose in describing the undergraduate's appearance and mannerisms in the first verse and the objects of his hatred in the second verse?

What is the role of Goole in this poem? Does his cynicism in any way stem from a feeling of the limitations imposed on him as a teacher by society's concept of what the end-product of a university education should be? ('Wanting to get out and earn... respected ... feared ... a place in the world')

Do you think that Philip Hobsbaum, in the last verse, is critical of the methods of university education in terms of their failure to produce what society demands of university education or is he critical of the fact that the demands of society pervert the ideal educational aims of a university education? What, then, seem to be Hobsbaum's feelings towards the attitudes revealed by the provincial undergraduate whom he portrays here?

For an interesting parallel view, see David Holbrook's poem entitled 'Living? Our Supervisors Will Do That For Us!'

The Ballad of Charlotte Dymond

*Charlotte Dymond, a domestic servant aged eighteen, was murdered near
Rowtor Ford on Bodmin Moor on Sunday, 14 April 1844, by her young
man, a crippled farm-hand, Matthew Weeks, aged twenty-two. A stone
marks the spot.*

It was a Sunday evening
    And in the April rain
That Charlotte went from our house
    And never came home again.

Her shawl of diamond redcloth,
    She wore a yellow gown,
She carried the green gauze handkerchief
    She bought in Bodmin town.

About her throat her necklace
    And in her purse her pay:
The four silver shillings
    She had at Lady Day.

In her purse four shillings
    And in her purse her pride
As she walked out one evening
    Her lover at her side.

Out beyond the marshes
    Where the cattle stand,
With her crippled lover
    Limping at her hand.

Charlotte walked with Matthew
    Through the Sunday mist,
Never saw the razor
    Waiting at his wrist.

Charlotte she was gentle
    But they found her in the flood
Her Sunday beads among the reeds
    Beaming with her blood.

Matthew, where is Charlotte,
　　And wherefore has she flown?
For you walked out together
　　And now are come alone.

Why do you not answer,
　　Stand silent as a tree,
Your Sunday worsted stockings
　　All muddied to the knee?

Why do you mend your breast-pleat
　　With a rusty needle's thread
And fall with fears and silent tears
　　Upon your single bed?

Why do you sit so sadly
　　Your face the colour of clay
And with a green gauze handkerchief
　　Wipe the sour sweat away?

Has she gone to Blisland
　　To seek an easier place,
And is that why your eye won't dry
　　And blinds your bleaching face?

'Take me home!' cried Charlotte,
　　'I lie here in the pit!
A red rock rests upon my breasts
　　And my naked neck is split!'

Her skin was soft as sable,
　　Her eyes were wide as day,
Her hair was blacker than the bog
　　That licked her life away.

Her cheeks were made of honey,
　　Her throat was made of flame
Where all around the razor
　　Had written its red name.

As Matthew turned to Plymouth
　　About the tilting Hoe,
The cold and cunning Constable
　　Up to him did go:

'I've come to take you, Matthew,
    Unto the Magistrate's door.
Come quiet now, you pretty poor boy,
    And you must know what for.'

'She is as pure,' cried Matthew,
    'As is the early dew,
Her only stain it is the pain
    That round her neck I drew!

'She is as guiltless as the day
    She sprang forth from her mother.
The only sin upon her skin
    Is that she loved another.'

They took him off to Bodmin,
    They pulled the prison bell,
They sent him smartly up to Heaven
    And dropped him down to Hell.

All through the granite kingdom
    And on its travelling airs
Ask which of these two lovers
    The most deserves your prayers.

And your steel heart search, Stranger,
    That you may pause and pray
For lovers who come not to bed
    Upon their wedding day,

But lie upon the moorland
    Where stands the sacred snow
Above the breathing river,
    And the salt sea-winds go.

Charles Causley

Porphyria's Lover

The rain set early in to-night,
    The sullen wind was soon awake,
It tore the elm-tops down for spite,
    And did its worst to vex the lake:
    I listened with heart fit to break.
When glided in Porphyria; straight
    She shut the cold out and the storm,
And kneeled and made the cheerless grate
    Blaze up, and all the cottage warm;
    Which done, she rose, and from her form
Withdrew the dripping cloak and shawl,
    And laid her soiled gloves by, untied
Her hat and let the damp hair fall,
    And, last, she sat down by my side
    And called me. When no voice replied,
She put my arm about her waist,
    And made her smooth white shoulder bare,
And all her yellow hair displaced,
    And, stooping, made my cheek lie there,
    And spread, o'er all, her yellow hair,
Murmuring how she loved me – she
    Too weak, for all her heart's endeavour,
To set its struggling passion free
    From pride, and vainer ties dissever,
    And give herself to me for ever.
But passion sometimes would prevail,
    Nor could to-night's gay feast restrain
A sudden thought of one so pale
    For love of her, and all in vain:
    So, she was come through wind and rain.
Be sure I looked up at her eyes
    Happy and proud; at last I knew
Porphyria worshipped me; surprise
    Made my heart swell, and still it grew
    While I debated what to do.
That moment she was mine, mine, fair,
    Perfectly pure and good: I found
A thing to do, and all her hair
    In one long yellow string I wound
    Three times her little throat around,
And strangled her. No pain felt she;
    I am quite sure she felt no pain.

As a shut bud that holds a bee,
    I warily oped her lids: again
    Laughed the blue eyes without a stain.
And I untightened next the tress
    About her neck; her cheek once more
Blushed bright beneath my burning kiss:
    I propped her head up as before,
    Only, this time my shoulder bore
Her head, which droops upon it still:
    The smiling rosy little head,
So glad it has its utmost will,
    That all it scorned at once is fled,
    And I, its love, am gained instead!
Porphyria's love: she guessed not how
    Her darling one wish would be heard.
And thus we sit together now,
    And all night long we have not stirred,
    And yet God has not said a word!

Robert Browning

NOTES

The Ballad of Charlotte Dymond

Charles Causley is a native of the Cornish town of Launceston
which lies on the eastern edge of Bodmin Moor.

Why is his use of the simple style of the old ballads so apt for
the telling of this type of true story? What in particular is achieved
here by the *starkness* of the style? To what extent does the use of
the ballad form with its short, terse lines and verses enable
Charles Causley to emphasise the full horror of the tragedy? In
what ways is he, nevertheless, able to *manipulate* detail – using
carefully chosen words and images – within these confines so that
his ballad becomes not just a plain narrative poem but an expression of his own individuality as a *poet*? How does he, during his
narrative, prepare the ground for his readers to ponder on the
thoughts of the last three verses?

Porphyria's Lover

This isn't a true story but the details have a very disturbing intimacy which makes the account of Porphyria's death seem appallingly real. How does Browning achieve this? What impressions of Porphyria's lover are conveyed in ways only possible through first person narrative, and why is the narrative style particularly apt here? What impressions are created by the narrator's calm, detailed appraisal of the events at the cottage? How does Browning convey to his readers that additional sense of horror which comes when the insanity of the killer is felt to be more disturbing than the actual moments of killing? How does the narrative style subtly reveal the narrator's mental state? What did he seek to achieve, at that moment, by strangling Porphyria?

Do these two poems share any common ground? What seem to be the intentions of the two poets in treating the subjects of their poems and how do their intentions fundamentally differ? In what ways do both poems illuminate darker aspects of love and jealousy through their *poetry* and in a manner not attainable in *prose*?

Encouragements to a Lover

Why so pale and wan, fond lover?
    Prythee, why so pale?
Will, when looking well can't move her,
    Looking ill prevail?
    Prythee, why so pale?

Why so dull and mute, young sinner?
    Prythee, why so mute?
Will, when speaking well can't win her,
    Saying nothing do't?
    Prythee, why so mute?

Quit, quit, for shame! this will not move,
    This cannot take her;
If of herself she will not love,
    Nothing can make her:
    The devil take her!

Sir John Suckling

Love in a Life

I

Room after room,
I hunt the house through
We inhabit together.
Heart, fear nothing, for, heart, thou shalt find her –
Next time, herself! – not the trouble behind her
Left in the curtain, the couch's perfume!
As she brushed it, the cornice-wreath blossomed anew:
Yon looking-glass gleamed at the wave of her feather.

II

Yet the day wears,
And door succeeds door;
I try the fresh fortune –
Range the wide house from the wing to the centre.
Still the same chance! she goes out as I enter.
Spend my whole day in the quest – who cares?
But 't is twilight, you see – with such suites to explore,
Such closets to search, such alcoves to importune!

Robert Browning

Life in a Love

Escape me?
Never –
Beloved!
While I am I, and you are you,
    So long as the world contains us both,
    Me the loving and you the loth,
While the one eludes, must the other pursue.
My life is a fault at last, I fear:
    It seems too much like a fate, indeed!
    Though I do my best I shall scarce succeed.
But what if I fail of my purpose here?
It is but to keep the nerves at strain,
    To dry one's eyes and laugh at a fall,
And, baffled, get up and begin again, –
    So the chase takes up one's life, that's all.
While, look but once from your farthest bound
    At me so deep in the dust and dark,
No sooner the old hope goes to ground
    Than a new one, straight to the self-same mark,
    I shape me –
    Ever
    Removed!

Robert Browning

Symptoms of Love

Love is a universal migraine,
A bright stain on the vision
Blotting out reason.

Symptoms of true love
Are leanness, jealousy,
Laggard dawns;

Are omens and nightmares –
Listening for a knock,
Waiting for a sign:

For a touch of her fingers
In a darkened room,
For a searching look.

Take courage, lover!
Could you endure such grief
At any hand but hers?

Robert Graves

NOTES

Encouragements to a Lover

Sir John Suckling (1609–42) was one of a group of seventeenth-century writers sometimes referred to as 'the cavalier poets', loyal to King Charles I and associated for the most part with the writing of short love poems both serious and lighthearted. What is the mood of *this* poem? What effects are produced by the presentation of the first two verses in the form of questions and by the change from question to exclamation in the third verse? What impression does the poem give to suggest that the man whom the poet is addressing is perhaps involved in the superficial *sensations* of being in love rather than in the deeper emotions of *loving*?

Love in a Life *and* Life in a Love

This pair of poems was written by the happily married Robert Browning in the mid-nineteenth century. In what ways do the poems complement each other? Why would either poem to some extent lose by being printed on its own? What impressions do both poems give to suggest that Browning is writing about a much deeper relationship than that implied in Suckling's poem? Why do *associations* rather than *sensations* produce the feeling in 'Love in a Life'? What effects are produced by the use of words such as 'escape', 'eludes', 'pursue', 'chase' and 'bound' in 'Life in a Love'? What contrasts are produced by Browning's writing about 'she' and 'I' in the first poem but addressing his beloved directly in the second poem? How do the titles of the two poems both sum up their complementary natures and reflect their contents?

Symptoms of Love

This is a twentieth century poem about love. Are there any similarities in attitude between this and Suckling's poem? What effect is achieved by describing love as a 'migraine' and by referring to 'symptoms'? In what ways, perhaps, does this poem probe a little more deeply into feelings than Suckling's poem (look at the third and fourth verses of this poem), and what are the very different implications of the addresses to the lover in the last verse of this poem and of Suckling's poem?

What essential differences are there between these four poems and Laurie Lee's 'First Love' on page 21?

The Ruined Maid

'O 'Melia, my dear, this does everything crown!
Who could have supposed I should meet you in Town?
And whence such fair garments, such prosperi – ty?' –
'O didn't you know I'd been ruined?' said she.

– 'You left us in tatters, without shoes or socks,
Tired of digging potatoes, and spudding up docks;
And now you've gay bracelets and bright feathers three!' –
'Yes: that's how we dress when we're ruined,' said she.

– 'At home in the barton[1] you said "thee" and "thou",
And "thik oon," and "theas oon," and "t'other"; but now
Your talking quite fits 'ee for high compa – ny!' –
'Some polish is gained with one's ruin,' said she.

– 'Your hands were like paws then, your face blue and bleak
But now I'm bewitched by your delicate cheek,
And your little gloves fit as on any la – dy!' –
'We never do work when we're ruined,' said she.

– 'You used to call home-life a hag-ridden dream,
And you'd sigh, and you'd sock; but at present you seem
To know not of megrims[2] or melancho – ly!' –
'True. One's pretty lively when ruined,' said she.

– 'I wish I had feathers, a fine sweeping gown,
And a delicate face, and could strut about Town!' –
'My dear – a raw country girl, such as you be,
Cannot quite expect that. You ain't ruined,' said she.

Thomas Hardy

---

[1] farm-yard
[2] low spirits

The Farmer's Bride

Three Summer since I chose a maid,
Too young maybe – but more's to do
At harvest-time than bide and woo.
    When us was wed she turned afraid
Of love and me and all things human;
Like the shut of a winter's day
Her smile went out, and 'twadn't a woman –
    More like a little frightened fay.[1]
    One night, in the Fall, she runned away.

'Out 'mong the sheep, her be,' they said,
'Should properly have been abed;
But sure enough she wadn't there
Lying awake with her wide brown stare.
So over seven-acre field and up-along across the down
We chased her, flying like a hare
Before our lanterns. To Church-Town
    All in a shiver and a scare
We caught her, fetched her home at last
    And turned the key upon her, fast.

She does the work about the house
As well as most, but like a mouse:
    Happy enough to chat and play
    With birds and rabbits and such as they,
    So long as men-folk keep away.

'Not near, not near!' her eyes beseech
When one of us comes within reach.
    The women say that beasts in stall
    Look round like children at her call.
    I've hardly heard her speak at all.

Shy as a leveret, swift as he,
Straight and slight as a young larch tree,
Sweet as the first wild violets, she,
To her wild self. But what to me?

The short days shorten and the oaks are brown,
    The blue smoke rises to the low grey sky,
One leaf in the still air falls slowly down,
    A magpie's spotted feathers lie
On the black earth spread white with rime,
The berries redden up to Christmas-time.
    What's Christmas-time without there be
    Some other in the house than we!

    She sleeps up in the attic there
    Alone, poor maid. 'Tis but a stair
Betwixt us. Oh! my God! the down,
The soft young down of her, the brown,
The brown of her – her eyes, her hair, her hair!

Charlotte Mew

[1] fairy

NOTES

The Ruined Maid

Brought up in a remote Dorset hamlet and the son of a stone-mason, Thomas Hardy was well aware of the limited horizons facing agricultural workers, men and women, in the nineteenth century. Hardy was fortunate enough to become apprenticed to a Dorchester architect and this led on to his spending a period in London as an assistant architect. This poem was written during this period, when Hardy was experiencing fashionable city life for himself. It is a light-heartedly ironic variation on a favourite Victorian theme, that of the innocent rural girl seduced by the local squire or squire's son and then abandoned. (Try to find a copy of the words of a well-known song of the time, 'She Was Poor But She Was Honest'.) Here, however, the 'ruined maid' has been taken up by her seducer and now leads a comfortable and fashionable life 'in Town'.

What hints are there in the poem that 'Melia may have allowed herself to be 'ruined' in order to get away from her labouring existence? What is gained by Hardy's casting the poem in the form of a dialogue? Why, perhaps, is 'Melia given the least to say? What appears to be Hardy's attitude towards 'Melia's behaviour?

The Farmer's Bride

What differences do you find between the characters and tempera-
ments of the 'farmer's bride' and the 'ruined maid' and between
the moods of this poem and Hardy's poem?

What evidence is there in Charlotte Mew's poem of the girl's
mental instability or – possibly – insanity, and of a fear of sex?
Why is stress laid on her affinity with animals, birds, and, even,
plants? Is there any suggestion that the farmer has any pity for the
girl's plight? What does he reveal of his self-pity, his passion, and
his lack of sensitivity towards – or perception of – what is really
wrong in his having married the girl? What seem to have been his
motives for marrying her? In what ways does the tragic nature of
the situation emerge from the narrative style of Charlotte Mew's
poem?

Did the very isolation of the lives of people living in rural
communities until the relatively recent past perhaps help to contribute to the incidence of psychologically incompatible or of love-
less marriages?

First Child

What fed their apprehension was the fears
Of loud compulsory insomnia,
Their little liberties abruptly cancelled,
The marvel of their marriage darkening
Beneath a wagging, sanitary bunting:
All these intrusions they would have to face.
But when the niggling interdicts and chill
Labours took up threatened residence
These seemed to be quite friendly after all.

What they had not prepared themselves to meet
Was this: the soft catastrophes, the sly
Menaces whose names are hard to spell
Creeping to her cot, the quiet killers
Loading their white guns and brooding over
That innocent and O, so fragile head.

Vernon Scannell

Early Morning Feed

The father darts out on the stairs
To listen to that keening
In the upper room, for a change of note
That signifies distress, to scotch disaster,
The kettle humming in the room behind.

He thinks, on tiptoe, ears a-strain,
The cool dawn rising like the moon:
'Must not appear and pick him up;
He mustn't think he has me springing
To his beck and call,'
The kettle rattling behind the kitchen door.

He has him springing
A-quiver on the landing –
For a distress-note, a change of key,
To gallop up the stairs to him
To take him up, light as a violin,
And stroke his back until he smiles.
He sidles in the kitchen
And pours his tea ...

And again stands hearkening
For milk cracking the lungs.
There's a little panting,
A cough: the thumb's in: he'll sleep,
The cup of tea cooling on the kitchen table.

Can he go in now to his chair and think
Of the miracle of breath, pick up a book,
Ready at all times to take it at a run
And intervene between him and disaster,
Sipping his cold tea as the sun comes up?

He returns to bed
And feels like something, with the door ajar,
Crouched in the bracken, alert, with big eyes
For the hunter, death, disaster.

Peter Redgrove

Married Evening

I watch his angular boned face
nod to the music, and his eyes
condone the gentle firelight.
My body sings. One nerve, it whines
stretched where he places it, in this hooded chair
opposite his. Around me all
my frittering words are graces to his peace
and wind among the notes, and with them seek
a formal close. Wry and alert
he asks about my day, and nods again
to expected cadences. I say
I took them walking in the fields
and watched them play, and leaned against
a stile, and looked to where cathedral spires
made gentle outlines, and their stretched bronze flags
jutted eternally one way in the sky.
Lying tonight beside him as he sleeps
my sweating self will suffer with the truth,
how stepping beyond the city boundary
is more momentous weekly; how today
my children scattered from my hands headlong
down runaway and many-acred slopes, and I

was desolate again, entire, as wind
ungroomed my hair, and spread its young girl's grace
over my cheeks, and brought back memories
of space and hope and possibilities
long lost. Tonight, I'll grip again
the spongey stile, and call my children back
and fill my hands with them, and ballast me
for the eternal journey home, I'll turn
to wake him, but will not, knowing how
I'd flounder, seeing alarm negate
the order he believes in, the control
by which he lives, by which I am defined.

Brian Jones

NOTES

First Child

The shape of this poem is vital to its subject matter, which is
concerned with assumed and actual fears associated with the
arrival of a first child. Notice how the shorter second section creates in the reader an almost parallel state of unpreparedness
which focuses attention on the *real* fears surrounding the early life
of the child. The unpreparedness is the more effectively under-
lined because of the similar structures which open each section
('What fed their apprehension was...' and 'What they had not
prepared themselves to meet was this:') and because the colon
which *follows* the list of assumed fears in the first section *precedes*
the list of actual fears in the second section, creating an early,
sudden pause in the movement and drawing attention to what
follows.

   In what ways do individual details stress the contrasts between the almost comfortable and certainly manageable appre-
hensions of the first section and the insidious and real fears
of the second section? What are the 'soft catastrophes', 'sly
menaces' and 'quiet killers', do you think?

Early Morning Feed

What common ground exists between this poem and 'First Child'? Once again a sense of unease pervades the latter part of the poem. How does Peter Redgrove convey this sense of unease? What effect is achieved by the use of the image of the hunter and the hunted in the last verse? What would appear to be the purpose of the references to the kettle and the tea? Sounds and movements are significant in this poem. Why, do you think? Look separately at the implications of these and at the tensions created by the progressions from 'humming' to 'rattling' and from 'darts' to 'springing' to 'gallop'. What is suggested by the use of the word 'sidles' and why is 'hearkening' particularly apt in its context?

In the first verse are two words particularly worth considering for their indirect as well as direct meanings. Consider the possible reasons for the use of 'keening' (rather than 'crying') and of 'scotch' (rather than, say, 'prevent').

Married Evening

Like 'Early Morning Feed' this sensitive poem reveals a certain unease in its contemplations of a different aspect of parenthood — that of the young mother whose husband is unaware of the special kind of loneliness which she experiences. What important similarities does Brian Jones establish between the music the husband is listening to and the 'music' of his wife's account of her day with the children? Why does he find his wife's 'frittering words' as relaxing and reassuring as the music? What significant differences emerge between the way the wife describes her day to her husband and her private thoughts as she lies in bed? Why doesn't she reveal these thoughts to her husband? Why does she find that 'stepping beyond the city boundary is more momentous weekly' and what might the 'memories of space and hope and possibilities long lost' be? What special effect is achieved in this poem by the use of first person narrative?

In what ways does the art of *poetry* in all three poems produce a more intense, direct contact with some of the more sensitive aspects of parenthood than would be possible in a prose treatment of these aspects?

Catkins

One of a thousand dust-blown, touchy
Shrubs in high summer, the catkin in March
Is a nettle of veins in a white eyeball
Pricked red against the ghost birch-wood and flooded farmland.

Here, where the hills begin
Is catkin country. Up this old cart-road
Shaking our city springs, tumbling the windscreen
High and low, as if the car were a wounded

Bird trying to keep aloft_of the flood –
The wiry, March-stiff catkin waits
Like fate for the open pen-knife –
The blade's squeak, the snap, and a branch of moth-soft buds.

We promised to bring her catkins,
Nothing else. But the cold that entered with us
Felt white, bloodless, in the hospital room. The furry buds
Would not stir. Our heat lay at their lost roots, and with hers.

David Wevill

Patients in a Public Ward

Like children now, bed close to bed,
With flowers set up where toys would be
In real childhoods, secretly
We cherish each our own disease,
And when we talk we talk to please
Ourselves that still we are not dead.

All is kept safe – the healthy world
Held at a distance, on a rope,
Where human things like hate and hope
Persist. The world we know is full
Of things we need, unbeautiful
And yet desired – a glass to hold

And sip, a cube of ice, a pill
To help us sleep. Yet in this warm
And sealed-off nest, the least alarm
Speaks clear of death. Our fears grow wide;
There are no places left to hide
And no more peace in lying still.

Elizabeth Jennings

NOTES

Catkins

For centuries poets have found symbols of various conditions of
human life in the seasons, the weather, fauna and flora. These
symbols can be particularly dramatic when they appear to reflect
something in one's own life. In this poem the cutting of catkins to
take to a patient in hospital appears to take on a symbolic significance. How is this significance reflected in David Wevill's
observation that the catkin 'waits like fate for the open pen-knife –
the blade's squeak, the snap...'? Why did the catkins seem to
bring cold into the hospital room – 'white, bloodless'? Why does
the writer (a father, with his children, visiting mother?) then note
that 'the furry buds would not stir'? Does the answer lie in the
final statement linking 'their lost roots' with 'hers' – and, if so,
what might her 'lost roots' be?

Patients in a Public Ward

In what ways does this poem suggest that Elizabeth Jennings is
writing from personal experience? What aspects of an adult patient's behaviour and outlook in hospital are illuminated by
Elizabeth Jennings's comparisons with aspects of childhood? How
does she perhaps hint that the combination of life in a hospital
ward and the state of being ill narrows feelings and needs to a
primitive, animal-like perspective?

Do the thoughts of these two poems complement each other in
any way?

Vital

I think my work is important, I am a link
In a long chain.
I had to have the training for it,
And I had to dirty my hands.
They ask my advice when they want to know what would be best.
I might move up even higher, in time.

One Sunday, I woke up shouting. She said,
What on earth's the matter, we're supposed to be
Going out to dinner later; or rather lunch
I dressed, and played with Lynda, and
Felt a bit better.

I was called into the office from the shop
Floor. 'Mr Fletton, up from London, wants to see you.'
But I was hearing the mutter-mutter,
The kind-of-giggling noises inside the machines
Through four thick concrete walls.
I could not read the words in front of my eyes.

She said last Thursday, you haven't said a thing
The whole evening.
I said no, I've been watching.
. . . I couldn't name a thing I'd seen on the screen.

Today is vital, people are relying on me
To get ten thousand packages out on time.
I am part of a chain, a link, they ask my advice.
I open the front door. After the wind,
It's a lovely cool morning, and sun;
Very bright.
The keys of the Toledo[1] are clenched wet
In my right hand. And I don't move.
I am standing shaking. I am standing, shaking.

Alan Brownjohn

[1] a small family car of the 1970s

The Suicide

And this, ladies and gentlemen, whom I am not in fact
Conducting, was his office all those minutes ago,
This man you never heard of. There are the bills
In the intray, the ash in the ashtray, the grey memoranda stacked
Against him, the serried ranks of the box-files, the packed
Jury of his unanswered correspondence
Nodding under the paperweight in the breeze
From the window by which he left; and here is the cracked
Receiver that never got mended and here is the jotter
With his last doodle which might be his own digestive tract
Ulcer and all or might be the flowery maze
Through which he had wandered deliciously till he stumbled
Suddenly conscious of all he lacked
On a manhole under the hollyhocks. The pencil
Point had obviously broken, yet, when he left this room
By catdrop sleight-of-foot or simple vanishing act,
To those who knew him for all that mess in the street,
This man with the shy smile has left behind
Something that was intact.

Louis MacNeice

The Psychiatrist Speaks

Quietly, patiently I wait
(And sometimes gently probe and peer)
To find the love, the lust, the hate,
The wound, the mystery, the fear
Within the mind-within-the-mind:
The mind that's like a face behind
A window curtain seeing unseen,
The mind that's wiser than you know,
The mind that says the things you mean,
The mind that's swift when you are slow,
The mind that wakes when daylight mind
Sleeps – and that sees when the other's blind,
The mind that has no 'good' or 'ill',
The mind that seems to lie so still
But moves calm-surely to its goal
As compass-needle moves to pole.

And then – when I (or rather you)
Have found the last and deepest clue,
The hate you hate, the fear you fear,
The worm that lies beneath the stone,
The ghost in that one room alone
Whose door you never dare unlock,
The secret you've forgotten so
Successfully so long ago
(And yet it's in that ticking clock,
It's on your track behind your back
Slowly, invisibly drawing near,
Softly preparing to attack) –
Then I say, 'Learn at last to live
Without your sackcloth, to forgive
Yourself the innocent sin, to cast
The burden of guilt away at last.'

A. S. J. Tessimond

NOTES

Vital

With considerable ingenuity Alan Brownjohn makes this poem reflect the state of mind of its narrator, a man who has found the pressures of his job too great for him and who is clearly in the process of cracking up under the strain. Note the illusion the poem gives to the reader of having been buttonholed by this man who simply *has* to talk to somebody . . .

What effects are produced by the constant use of 'I' in the narrative, by the references to his wife as 'she', by the frequent switching between references to work and references to home? Why does Alan Brownjohn present the narrative in untidy and jerky sentence constructions and varying verse lengths? Is there any special significance in the title of the poem?

The Suicide

Louis MacNeice was himself no stranger to office life and this poem concerns the suicide of one of his colleagues. The violence of the suicide is relegated to a brief reference to 'all that mess in the street'; what MacNeice is more concerned with is an appraisal of the circumstances which led to the act, and he achieves this by examining significant details within the man's office.

In the hands of a poet seemingly trivial items of an inventory provide disturbing revelations, and each item is worth pondering. What special significance can you find in the use of the metaphors of 'serried ranks' and 'packed jury' of 'box-files' and 'unanswered correspondence', for instance? Why are the 'memoranda' 'grey' and what does the phrase 'stacked against him' imply? Why was the cracked receiver never mended and how did it come to be cracked? What does the image of 'the flowery maze through which he had wandered deliciously' indicate of the state of mind reflected in his doodling? What does 'a manhole under the hollyhocks' represent, and what did the man feel that he lacked? (Inspiration? Creativity?)

One is left with two mysteries – the beginning and the ending of the poem. Why does MacNeice start as if he is conducting a party round the dead man's office only to deny this – 'whom I am not in fact conducting'? Why 'ladies and gentlemen', then? And what *is* 'intact' that the man 'with the shy smile' has left behind?

Does the reading of this poem promote any additional reflections on the man who is the subject of the poem 'Vital'?

The Psychiatrist Speaks

The clarity of this poem seems to be achieved in the first section by means of a probing with words which enables the reader to grasp the significance of the role of the subconscious. Note the way in which Tessimond assembles a formidable list of qualities which at first appear to be familiar aspects of *conscious* thought (love, lust, hate...), only to emphasise their *real* existence 'within the mind-within-the-mind'. The colon which follows is in itself a dramatic gesture, a pause as the door into the subconscious is unlocked. It is the *subconscious* which is the dominating subject and which provides the opening words of no less than six of the lines which follow 'The mind that...'. The *'you'* of the *conscious* is significantly placed at the *end* of the line: 'The mind that's wiser than *you* know'.

How do the images of the face behind the curtain and the compass needle reinforce the psychiatrist's contentions? How is the sense of tension built up in the first section of the poem gradually released in the second section? Why is the resolution of the anticipatory 'And then' delayed to a point four lines from the end? What, according to the final statement in the poem, is the end product of successful psychoanalysis?

Does this poem promote any special reflections in relation to the poems 'The Suicide' and 'Vital'?

Poor Old Horse

A child skipping jump on the quay at the Mill,
With parted legs jump, soft-footed in April,
And the lovers on the bridge, sweet soft women's mouths
Pressing jowls of men, in jeans or loose trousers, youths
Packed in punts. And the masons on the bridge
Pause as they lift white stone to dress the face of the ridge
Of the balustrade, to imagine an actorish man
(Uxorious to a self-possessed blonde) as well as they can,
Back in the hotel room, making love; they laugh,
Turn back to the mortar. Ducks rise over trees, the chaff
Of mixed men and women floats over. A boy with a shiny red face
Attentively wipes some beer from his sweetheart's sleeve. The
       place
I remember assignments of old at, by moon and water,
The same acts of living, the same weir-splashed happiness after.
But today I sit here alone – with my daughter rather,
Who critically watches the child skipping jump on the waterfall
       quay,
And we after go back to the car. I am dumb, and silent she.
I see the spring love on the bridge for her: for me decay,
Or at the most the wry pretension, 'Well, we have had our day!'
I do not want to have had my day: I do not accept my jade,
Any more than the grey old horse we meet in the street,
His shaggy stiff dragged aside for a smart sports blade
And his smart sports car: yet that's no doubt my fate
As the water flows by here each year, April to April,
With a soft-footed child skipping jump on the quay at the Mill.

David Holbrook

Poetry of Departures

Sometimes you hear, fifth-hand,
An epitaph:
He chucked up everything
And just cleared off,
And always the voice will sound
Certain you approve
This audacious, purifying,
Elemental move.

And they are right, I think.
We all hate home
And having to be there:
I detest my room,
Its specially-chosen junk,
The good books, the good bed,
And my life, in perfect order:
So to hear it said

He walked out on the whole crowd
Leaves me flushed and stirred,
Like *Then she undid her dress*
Or *Take that you bastard*;
Surely I can, if he did?
And that helps me to stay
Sober and industrious.
But I'd go today,

Yes, swagger the nut-strewn roads,
Crouch in the fo'c'sle
Stubbly with goodness, if
It weren't so artificial,
Such a deliberate step backwards
To create an object:
Books; china; a life
Reprehensibly perfect.

Philip Larkin

NOTES

Poor Old Horse

In what ways is the poet's nostalgia for the Cambridge of his student days reflected in the poem? What is the special significance here of the presence of the skipping child and of his own daughter – and of its being April? What aspects of the poem would seem to indicate that its writer is approaching middle age? Why does David Holbrook include the reactions of the masons? What is the purpose of including the reference to 'the grey old horse' and what is the significance of the poem's title – bearing in mind that it is also the title of an old folk song, the words of which bear some relevance to the mood of this poem?

Poetry of Departures

'I do not want to have had my day,' exclaims David Holbrook in 'Poor Old Horse'. Holbrook's envy of youth in his poem may seem to be mainly sexual in its implication, but it is surely symptomatic of a more general apprehension of the moral and social *evenness* of middle age. How is a similar apprehension expressed in the second verse of Philip Larkin's poem? What aspects of boredom with established routine do the italicised statements deliberately evoke, and why might they have a powerful appeal to those who are bored with the flat landscapes of middle life? Why does Larkin describe the idea of chucking up everything as appearing, to some, an 'audacious, purifying, elemental move'? What are Larkin's ultimate reasons for rejecting the delights offered in the four statements? Do you find Larkin's conclusions in any way smug – or is he deliberately creating a condition of self-defence in which temptation is less likely to be effective if one addresses oneself to it in a patronising manner?

My Old Acquaintance

Working her toothless gums till her sharp chin
Could almost reach and touch her sharper nose,
These are the words my old acquaintance said:
'I have four children, all alive and well;
My eldest girl was seventy years in March,
And though when she was born her body was
Covered all over with black hair, and long
Which when I saw at first made me cry out,
"Take it away, it is a monkey – ugh!"
Yet she's as smooth and fair as any, now.
And I, who sit for hours in this green space
That has seven currents of good air, and pray
At night to Jesus and his Mother, live
In hopes to reach my ninetieth year in June.
But ere it pleases God to take my soul,
I'll sell my fine false teeth, which cost five pounds,
Preserved in water now for twenty years,
For well I know these girls will fight for them
As soon as I am near my death; before
My skin's too cold to feel the feet of flies.
God bless you and good day – I wish you well.
For me, I cannot relish food, or sleep
Till God sees fit to hold the Kaiser fast,
Stabbed, shot, or hanged – and his black soul
Sent into hell, to bubble, burn and squeal;
Think of the price of fish – and look at bacon!'

W. H. Davies

The Light of Other Days

Oft in the stilly night
   Ere slumber's chain has bound me,
Fond Memory brings the light
   Of other days around me:
      The smiles, the tears
      Of boyhood's years,
   The words of love then spoken;
      The eyes that shone,
      Now dimm'd and gone,
   The cheerful hearts now broken!
Thus in the stilly night
   Ere slumber's chain has bound me,
Sad Memory brings the light
   Of other days around me.

When I remember all
   The friends so link'd together
I've seen around me fall
   Like leaves in wintry weather,
      I feel like one
      Who treads alone
   Some banquet-hall deserted,
      Whose lights are fled,
      Whose garlands dead,
   And all but he departed!
Thus in the stilly night
   Ere slumber's chain has bound me,
Sad Memory brings the light
   Of other days around me.

Thomas Moore

Old Woman

So much she caused she cannot now account for
As she stands watching day return, the cool
Walls of the house moving towards the sun.
She puts some flowers in a vase and thinks
    'There is not much I can arrange
In here and now, but flowers are suppliant

As children never were. And love is now
A flicker of memory, my body is
My own entirely. When I lie at night
I gather nothing now into my arms,
    No child or man, and where I live
Is what remains when men and children go.'

Yet she owns more than residue of lives
That she has marked and altered. See how she
Warns time from too much touching her possessions
    By keeping flowers fed by polishing
        Her fine old silver. Gratefully
She sees her own glance printed on grandchildren.

Drawing the curtains back and opening windows
Every morning now, she feels her years
Grow less and less. Time puts no burden on
Her now she does not need to measure it.
    It is acceptance she arranges
And her own life she places in the vase.

Elizabeth Jennings

NOTES

My Old Acquaintance

The references to the Kaiser and to food prices help to date the old lady's monologue to the period of the First World War, when the German Emperor ('Kaiser') drew the sort of intense hatred which Britain directed towards Hitler in the Second World War.

Many television documentaries employ the technique of self-revelation by eliminating the questions of interviewers and allowing people to express their views at length, apparently spontaneously. Here, as in such television documentaries, self-revelation by the character *may* also be a reflection of the attitudes of the artist who arranged and, possibly, edited it. What aspects of the 'old acquaintance' probably appealed to W. H. Davies sufficiently for him to be moved to write this poem? How does he achieve a realistic, intimate contact between the old lady and his readers? What does the old lady reveal of herself in her monologue?

This is a poem of encounter in which the impact on the poet of a meeting with a specific character on a specific occasion provides the matter for a poem. Sometimes, however, the poet deliberately uses an encounter in order to illustrate openly his own outlooks or philosophy. A good example of this, and a vivid narrative of an encounter with a man 'in his extreme old age', is Wordsworth's poem 'Resolution and Independence', the result of a meeting with a leech-gatherer in the Lake District – a meeting also recalled by Wordsworth's sister Dorothy in her Grasmere Journals.

The Light of Other Days

This poem about old age has to be considered in a special context; its author, Thomas Moore (1779–1852), was an eminent Irish poet and musician, and a number of his poems, this among them, became famous as songs. What aspects of the structure of this poem suggest the intention of writing a lyric which could easily be set to music? Moore's songs were especially popular in the nineteenth century at family musical evenings. In what ways is the imagery of this poem aptly sentimental for such evenings and how is it helped by the rhythm of the poem? Do you feel that Moore has calculated the effects in this poem so that it moves rather than disturbs?

What differences do you find between the mood of evocation

of the past in this poem and the mood of the reminiscences in 'My Old Acquaintance'? Are these differences wholly due to the different purposes and the different periods of writing of the poets, or is the sentimentality of Thomas Moore's poem typical of an old man rather than an old woman?

Old Woman

Thomas Moore evokes only a self-indulgent sorrowing for old age which possesses a mild element of pleasure in tearfulness. Elizabeth Jennings makes a much cooler appraisal of old age. What makes it an infinitely more balanced and optimistic view than that presented in Tom Moore's poem? Like the catkins in David Wevill's poem (p. 46), flowers are central to this poem's meanings and implications. Why is the old woman's arranging of flowers of special significance here? What is suggested by the word 'arrange' in the first verse, and how does the word 'arranges' in the last verse come to carry a much deeper meaning? Why is the flower *vase* an important symbol?

How does Elizabeth Jennings's 'Old Woman' differ from W. H. Davies's 'My Old Acquaintance' and in what ways are the *intentions* of the two poets in presenting their characters very different?

Old Furniture

I know not how it may be with others
    Who sit amid relics of householdry
That date from the days of their mothers' mothers,
    But well I know how it is with me
        Continually.

I see then hands of the generations
    That owned each shiny familiar thing
In play on its knobs and indentations,
    And with its ancient fashioning
        Still dallying:

Hands behind hands, growing paler and paler,
    As in a mirror a candle-flame
Shows images of itself, each frailer
    As it recedes, though the eye may frame
        Its shape the same.

On the clock's dull dial a foggy finger,
    Moving to set the minutes right
With tentative touches that lift and linger
    In the wont of a moth on a summer night,
        Creeps to my sight.

On this old viol, too, fingers are dancing –
    As whilom[1] – just over the strings by the nut,
The tip of a bow receding, advancing
    In airy quivers, as if it would cut
        The plaintive gut.

And I see a face by that box for tinder,
    Glowing forth in fits from the dark,
And fading again, as the linten cinder
    Kindles to red at the flinty spark,
        Or goes out stark.

Well, well. It is best to be up and doing,
    The world has no use for one to-day
Who eyes things thus – no aim pursuing!
    He should not continue in this stay,
        But sink away.

Thomas Hardy

[1] formerly, once

The Caledonian Market

A work-basket made of an old armadillo
    Lined with pink satin now rotten with age,
A novel entitled *The Ostracized Vicar*
    (A spider squashed flat on the title-page),
A faded album of nineteen-oh-seven
    Snapshots (now like very weak tea)
Showing high collared knuts[1] and girls expectant
    In big muslin hats at Bexhill-on-Sea,
A gasolier[2] made of hand-beaten copper
    In the once modern style known as *art nouveau*,
An assegai,[3] and a china slipper,
    And *What a Young Scoutmaster Ought to Know* . . .

Who stood their umbrellas in elephants' feet?
    Who hung their hats on the horns of a moose?
Who crossed the ocean with amulets made
    To be hung round the neck of an ailing papoose?
Who paid her calls with a sandalwood card-case?
    From whose eighteen-inch waist hung that thin chatelaine?[4]
Who smoked that meerschaum?[5] Who won that medal?
    That extraordinary vase was evolved by what brain?
Who worked in wool the convolvulus bell pull?
    Who smiled with those false teeth? Who wore that wig?
Who had that hair-tidy hung by her mirror?
    Whose was that scent-bottle shaped like a pig?

Where are the lads in their tight Norfolk jackets
    Who roistered in pubs that stayed open all day?
Where are the girls in their much tighter corsets
    And where are the figures they loved to display?
Where the old maids in their bric-à-brac[6] settings
    With parlourmaids bringing them dinners and teas?
Where are their counterparts, idle old roués,[7]
    Sodden old bachelors living at ease?
Where the big families, big with possessions,
    Their standards of living, their errors of taste?
Here are the soup-tureens – where is the ambience,
    Arrogance, confidence, hope without haste?

Laugh if you like at this monstrous detritus[8]
    Of middle-class life in the liberal past,
The platypus stuffed, and the frightful epergne.[9]
    You, who are now overtaxed and declassed,

Laugh, while you can, for the time may come round
    When the rubbish you treasure will lie in this place –
Your wireless set (bust), your ridiculous hats,
    And the photographs of your period face.
Your best-selling novels, your 'functional' chairs,
    Your primitive comforts and notions of style
Are just so much fodder for dealers in junk –
    Let us hope that they'll make your grandchildren smile.

William Plomer

[1] dandies
[2] a frame to hold gas-burners
[3] an African spear
[4] an ornamental appendage worn by ladies at their waist, with short chains attached for keys, scissors, penknife, thimble-case, etc.
[5] a tobacco pipe made of meerschaum – a fine, light whitish clay
[6] antiquarian odds and ends
[7] men given to leading lives of sensual pleasure
[8] debris
[9] an ornamental centrepiece for the dinner table

Home

Home is so sad. It stays as it was left,
Shaped to the comfort of the last to go
As if to win them back. Instead, bereft[1]
Of anyone to please, it withers so,
Having no heart to put aside the theft

And turn again to what it started as,
A joyous shot at how things ought to be,
Long fallen wide. You can see how it was:
Look at the pictures and the cutlery.
The music in the piano stool. That vase.

Philip Larkin

[1] forcibly deprived (of)

NOTES

Old Furniture

In what ways does Hardy emphasise the tactile associations of the old furniture and what effect do these emphases have on the atmosphere of the poem? (It is worth noting that Hardy's father played the violin at local dances and that Hardy wrote a separate poem entitled 'To My Father's Violin'.)

What impression does Hardy create by his use of the very short last line for each verse? What does he reveal of his personal attitudes in the poem, both in his meditations on the furniture and in the change of mood in the final verse?

The Caledonian Market

The Caledonian Market remains London's famous market for old furniture and bric-à-brac, although it has now moved from its original site near King's Cross Station to Bermondsey, south of the Thames.

As the last verse, with its references to wireless sets and 'functional' chairs suggests, the poem was originally addressed to readers who lived through the 1930s, during which time the objects observed in the Caledonian Market by Plomer were generally regarded as 'junk'. Today some of them would have considerable antique value.

Note the way in which Plomer begins with an amusing list in the first verse ('A ... An ... A ... A') and then personalises the objects detailed in the second verse ('Who? ... Who?') before dwelling almost solely on people in the third verse ('Where? ... Where?'). How does this method of construction progressively restore and underline the personal associations which all these *objects* once possessed? What is Plomer's 'message' in the last verse and in what tone is it delivered, do you think? What is the general intention of the poem?

Home

The word 'bereft' might at first seem an intrusion of poetic diction
for the sake of a rhyme. Further investigation reveals that it is a
key to the meaning of the poem. As well as meaning 'forcibly
deprived' it is also defined as 'deprived of a near relation, be-
reaved'. Furthermore, the word 'bereave' also means 'rob'. To
catch the restrained poignancy of this poem, imagine that Philip
Larkin is conducting you inside a home deprived by death of its
last occupant. The home reflects the personality of that occupant;
deprived of that personality it assumes an increasingly desolate
appearance as dust collects, yet it never quite loses its personality
as long as objects – picture, vase, piano stool, music – remain in
position. At such a time a home can appear just as anthropomor-
phic (an impersonal object given human personality) as Larkin
suggests in the first verse of the poem. It *is* 'so sad' and it *does*
appear 'bereft'.

'Bereft of anyone to please': re-read Hardy's 'Old Furniture' in
the light of this observation, and then look again at the objects
displayed in William Plomer's 'The Caledonian Market'.

What final reflections do all three poems provide on the subject of domestic possessions?

Moving House

Like a life that dies on a summer's afternoon,
The blood in the veins of the house
Is weakening now. Was strong and thick
In the arteries, and thicker still
In the children's songs.
The inquisitive sun is sprinkling light
On the chairs, the tables, the cups and plates,
And the strange black van that is waiting.

There were doors in the house that opened
Only at times, for the keys were lost.
But the other doors swung on their hinges
And the rooms became worn to the shape
Of the lives that fitted them.

There were faces that drifted out of the mists
Surrounding us, stayed for a time, became
Part of the mood that was governing us.
Now are blurred into the cherry tree's flowering,
Or preserved in a dream that recurs.

Now the rooms are all disordered by emptiness,
Sudden exposure of dust and paint that is peeling.
In the drive an armchair sags in the sunlight,
And holly and yew are sheltering things
Like displaced persons, all huddled and bruised
Waiting their next rough handling.

Heather Buck

Leady-Day, an' Ridden House

Aye, back at Leady-Day, you know,
O come vrom Gullybrook to Stowe;
At Leady-Day I took my pack
O' rottletraps, an' turn'd my back
Upon the weather-beaten door,
That had a-screen'd, so long avore,
The mwost that thease zide o' the greave,
I'd live to have, or die to seave!
My childern, an' my vier-pleace,
Where Molly wi' her cheerful feace,
When I'd a-trod my wat'ry road
Vrom night-bedarden'd vields abrode,
Wi' nimble hands, at evenen, blest
Wi' vire an' vood my hard-won rest;
The while the little woones did clim'
So sleek-skinn'd, up from lim' to lim',
Till, strugglen hard an' clingen tight,
They reach'd at last my feace's height.
All tryen which could soonest hold
My mind wi' little teales they twold.
An' ridden house is such a caddle.[1]
I shan't be over keen vor mwore o't,
Nor yet a while, you mid be sure o't, –
I'd rather keep to woone wold staddle.[2]

Well, zoo, avore the east begun
To redden wi' the comen zun,
We left the beds our mossy thatch
Wer never mwore to overstratch,
An' borrow'd uncle's wold hoss Dragon,
To bring the slowly lumbren waggon,
An' when he come, we vell a-packen
The bedsteads, wi' their rwopes and zacken;
An' then put up the wold earm-chair,
An' cwoffer vull ov e'then-ware,
An' vier-dogs, an' copper kittle,
Wi' crocks an' saucepans, big an' little;
An' fryen-pan, vor aggs to slide
In butter round his hissen zide,
An' gridire's even bars, to bear
The drippen steake above the gleare

O' brightly-glowen coals. An' then,
All up o' top o' them agean
The woaken bwoard, where we did eat
Our croust o' bread or bit o' meat, –
An' when the bwoard wer up, we tied
Upon the reaves,[3] along the zide,
The woaken stools, his glossy meates,
Bwoth when he's beare, or when the pleates
Do clatter loud wi' knives, below
Our merry feaces in a row.
An' put between his lags, turn'd up'ard,
The zalt-box an' the corner cupb'ard.
An' then we laid the wold clock-cease,
All dumb, athirt upon his feace,
Vor we'd a-left, I needen tell ye,
Noo works 'ithin his head or belly.
An' then we put upon the pack
The settle, flat upon his back;
An' after that, a-tied in pairs
In woone another, all the chairs,
An' bits o' lumber wo'th a ride,
An' at the very top a-tied,
The children's little stools did lie,
Wi' lags a-turn'd toward the sky:
Zoo there we lwoaded up our scroff,[4]
An' tied it vast, an' started off.
An', – as the waggon cooden car all
We had to teake, – the butter-barrel
An' cheese-wring, wi' his twinen screw,
An' all the pails an' veats,[5] an' blue
Wold milk leads, and a vew things mwore,
Wer all a-carr'd the day avore,
And when the mwost ov our wold stuff
Wer brought outside o' thik brown ruf,[6]
I rambled round wi' narrow looks,
In fusty holes an' darksome nooks,
To gather all I still mid vind,
O' rags or sticks a-left behind.
An' there the unlatch'd doors did creak,
A-swung by winds, a-streamen weak
Drough[7] empty rooms, an' meaken sad
My heart, where me'th woonce meade me glad.
Vor when a man do leave the he'th
An' ruf where vu'st he drew his breath,

Or where he had his bwoyhood's fun,
An' things wer woonce a-zaid an' done
That took his mind, do touch his heart
A little bit, I'll answer vor't.
Zoo ridden house is such a caddle,
That I would rather keep my staddle.

William Barnes

[1] a muddle, a puzzling plight

[2] a bed, or a frame for ricks

[3] the ladder-like framework attached to the sides of a waggon to hold up the load extended laterally over wheels.

[4] small bits of dead wood fallen under trees, or leavings under wood piles or faggots

[5] cheese vats

[6] roof

[7] through

Glenaradale

There is no fire of the crackling boughs
    On the hearth of our fathers,
There is no lowing of brown-eyed cows
    On the green meadows,
Nor do the maidens whisper vows
    In the still gloaming,
        Glenaradale.

There is no bleating of sheep on the hill
    Where the mists linger,
There is no sound of the low hand-mill
    Ground by the women,
And the smith's hammer is lying still
    By the brown anvil,
        Glenaradale.

Ah! we must leave thee and go away
    Far from Ben Luibh,
Far from the graves where we hoped to lay
    Our bones with our fathers',
Far from the kirk where we used to pray
    Lowly together,
        Glenaradale.

We are not going for hunger of wealth,
    For the gold and silver,
We are not going to seek for health
    On the flat prairies,
Nor yet for the lack of fruitful tilth
    On thy green pastures,
       Glenaradale.

Content with the croft and the hill were we,
    As all our fathers,
Content with the fish in the lake to be
    Carefully netted,
And garments spun of the wool from thee,
    O black-faced wether
       Of Glenaradale!

No father here but would give a son
    For the old country,
And his mother the sword would have girded on
    To fight her battles:
Many's the battle that has been won
    By the brave tartans,
       Glenaradale.

But the big-horn'd stag, and his hinds, we know,
    In the high corries,
And the salmon that swirls in the pool below
    Where the stream rushes
Are more than the hearts of men, and so
    We leave thy green valley,
       Glenaradale.

Walter C. Smith

NOTES

Moving House

Can you discover any similarities between Philip Larkin's 'Home'
– 'shaped to the comfort of the last to go' – and the references in
the first verse of this poem to 'the blood in the veins of the house
...weakening now' – 'blood' which *was* 'strong and thick in the

arteries'? What other similarities in *feelings* are there between the two poems?

What aspects of moving house, do you think, help to produce strong and sometimes disturbing feelings on the day one actually moves? What evidence is there of these strong and disturbing feelings in this poem, and in what ways does the poem suggest that it has been written from direct personal experience, possibly on the day of moving or soon afterwards? If you didn't know that the poem had been written by a woman would it suggest, in its treatment of the subject, that it represented a woman's view?

Leady-Day, an' Ridden House

What different emphases do you find between this account of moving house and that of Heather Buck in her poem 'Moving House'? What differences do there appear to be between the outlook of the narrator in Barnes's poem and the outlook of the observer in Heather Buck's poem? Are the differences in any way conditioned by the fact that one is a woman's poem and the other a man's poem? Are they conditioned in any way by the different period settings of the two poems?

The Anglican priest and Dorset dialect poet William Barnes (1801–86) was a farmer's son and his rural poetry reveals his close acquaintance with Dorset country life in the nineteenth century. Lady Day, 25 March, gained its name when it was one of four holy days associated with the Virgin Mary. It became one of four 'Quarter-Days', fixed by custom as marking the quarters of the year when tenancies of houses began and ended. In Dorset the Hiring Fair held at Candlemas (Feast of the Purification of the Virgin Mary) was a time for farm labourers to enter into new contracts for the twelve months following Lady Day, and this was a time when many labourers changed their jobs by attending the fair, held at the county town of Dorchester. In this poem Barnes conveys the calm stoicism of the farm worker in an account of the day of moving as the labourer would have experienced it.

Barnes also wrote many poems in standard English. What would you consider to be the special advantages of composing this poem in dialect, in terms of its effect on the reader? Is its effectiveness at all enhanced by the use of rhyming couplets? What evidence is there in the poem that this is the labourer's first move for many years and that it is therefore of considerable emotional significance to him? How does this significance convey a sense of pathos through the carefully tuned understatement of the narrative? What does the poem reveal of the functional nature of the furniture and equipment possessed by the agricultural workers' families? How does Barnes in this poem manage to identify so closely with the character and surroundings of the farm labourer that one seems to be in direct communication with the labourer without the intervening agency of the poet?

For a similar but more detailed account of Lady-Day home-movings in Dorset, see Chapter 52 of Hardy's novel *Tess of the D'Urbervilles*.

Glenaradale

There was considerable emigration of the population from the Highlands of Scotland following the defeat of the rebellion of Charles Edward Stuart in 1745 and the consequent reduction of the forces of armed men as the tribal system of the Clans lost its power. Emigrations continued to increase as sheep farming replaced corn growing and cattle rearing in the Highlands. Perhaps the greatest bitterness in connection with the continued depopulation of the Highlands came, however, later in the nineteenth century when many Highlanders were displaced from their homes to make way for the establishment of vast deer forests and grouse moors, an event known as 'the Highland Clearances'.

In this poem, Walter Chalmers Smith (1824–1908), a Scottish minister who became Moderator of the General Assembly of the Free Church of Scotland, writes of the human misery created by the Clearances. By what means in these verses does Walter Smith illustrate his own sense of social commitment to write the poem? What are the effects achieved, for instance, by the succession of negatives in the first two verses and by the repeated phrases elsewhere ('Far from . . .', 'We are not going . . .', 'Content . . .')? What examples of the deliberate use of emotive language do you find in the poem? To what extent is the use of emotive detail perhaps particularly designed to appeal to Scottish readers? Although Walter Smith effectively emphasises the distress created by the Clearances, his criticism of the purpose of the Clearances is discreetly implied in the final verse and the instigators of the Clearances remain unmarked. Why might this be, do you think?

The Gathering

Fast as the fatal symbol[1] flies,
In arms the huts and hamlets rise;
From winding glen, from upland brown,
They pour'd each hardy tenant down.
Nor slack'd the messenger his pace;
He show'd the sign, he named the place,
And, pressing forward like the wind,
Left clamour and surprise behind.
Till rose in arms each man might claim
A portion in Clan-Alpine's name,
From the grey sire, whose trembling hand
Could hardly buckle on his brand,
To the raw boy, whose shaft and bow
Were yet scarce terror to the crow.
Each valley, each sequester'd glen,
Muster'd its little horde of men,
That met as torrents from the height
In Highland dales their streams unite,
Still gathering, as they pour along,
A voice more loud, a tide more strong,
Till at the rendezvous they stood
By hundreds prompt for blows and blood;
Each train'd to arms since life began,
Owing no tie but to his clan,
No oath, but by his chieftain's hand,
No law, but Roderick Dhu's command.
A various scene the clansmen made,
Some sate, some stood, some slowly stray'd;
But most, with mantles folded round,
Were couch'd to rest upon the ground,
Scarce to be known by curious eye,
From the deep heather where they lie,
So well was match'd the tartan screen
With heath-bell dark and brackens green;
Unless where, here and there, a blade,
Or lance's point a glimmer made,
Like glow-worm twinkling through the shade.
But when, advancing through the gloom,
They saw the Chieftain's eagle plume,
Their shout of welcome, shrill and wide,
Shook the steep mountain's steady side.

Thrice it arose, and lake and fell
Three times return'd the martial yell;
It died upon Bochastle's plain,
And silence claim'd her evening reign.

Sir Walter Scott

(from the Third Canto of *The Lady of the Lake*)

[1] the 'fatal symbol' was a crosslet (a small cross) made of yew; its points were
dipped in the blood of a newly killed goat. It was a symbol of the clan leader's
summons to his clan. A messenger would visit all members of the clan, naming
the place of the gathering and displaying the crosslet. Failure to 'rear the ready
spear' in response to the 'fatal symbol' would result in speedy and bloody
vengeance!

At the Highland Games

Like re-reading a book which has lost its pith.

Watching the piper dandying over a sodden stage
saluting an empty tent.

The empty beer glasses catch the sun
sparkle like old brooches against green.

Fur-hatted, with his huge twirling silver stick
the pipe-major has gypsy cheekbones, colour of brick.

Everything drowses. The stewards with aloof eagle stare
sit on collapsing rock, chair on brown chair.

Once the pibroch showed the grave 'ground'
of seas without bubbles, where great hulks were drowned,

meat with moustaches. The heroic dead die
over and over the sea to misty Skye.

Past the phantom ivy, bird song, I walk
among crew-cuts, cameras, the heather-covered rock,

past my ancestry, peasant, men who bowed
with stony necks to the daughter-stealing lord.

Past my ancestry, the old songs, the pibroch
stirring my consciousness like the breeze a loch

Past my buried heart my friend who complains
of 'All the crime, their insane violence'.

Stone by stone the castles crumble. The seas
have stored away their great elegies.

'Morag of Dunvegan.' Dandy piper
with delicate soft paws, knee-bending stepper,

saluting an empty tent. Blue-kilted stewards
strut like strange storks along the sodden sward.

Finished. All of it's finished. The Gaelic
boils in mouth, the South Sea silver stick

twirls, settles. The mannequins are here.
Calum, how you'd talk of their glassy stare,

their loud public voices. Stained pictures
of what was raw, violent, alive and coarse.

I watch their heirs, Caligulas[1] with canes
stalk in their rainbow kilts towards the dance.

Iain Crichton Smith

[1] Gaius Caesar Caligula, a Roman emperor whose reign was characterised by
cruelty and vice. His name originated in his wearing *caligae* (soldier's boots)
when he was a boy.

Ancestors

If they had the sea in their blood,
what have we?
There's petrochemical in mine.
I shiver to recognize something of me
at Stevenston and Invergordon.
Their faded eyes, the photo-ancestors,
will meet in mine
the images of steel on stone, the still
of the created world.

I'd tear my own life clear
of these earlier lives
where they yielded
and were put to the sea,
like people, I imagine,
who decay on newsreel.

Their suffering
is in a body where the bones escape.
Sheep crop the scruff of this brown land.
The skeletons of little water mills
where burns drop
to an empty shore.
The six oared boat, frame giving way,
is shrouded by wrack.
Some bits of guillemot, a little oiled.
And that is all, this back end
of a century.

Fulmars take over the old croft houses.
A raucous confidence, fulmars
thriving. Peregrine falcon
back up on the hill,
smashed on our legal acids,
dropping painfully out
of this bare place.
A dying bird knows.
A winning one is aware.
Between the bird sense and the oil,
I begin to be doubtful:
> May the wild protect us
> from a stiffening of vision!
> May the wildness speak the right
> of people to their love,
> their past . . .
Their way too
was of acceptance, ancestors. My great
great grandfather spoke back to Sutherland.
'Na, Duke, I'm right. I'll not apologize.'
He was exceptional, then homeless.

I'm leaving the wild to itself.
The wheatear persuasion
(inside the dyke, a perfected nest).
The curlew urging
(her young merge into the ground).
The chorus reminding.
This country has been rich with them,
the birds that sing,
and those who are silent.

Robin Munro

NOTES

The Gathering

This passage comes from one of Sir Walter Scott's lengthy narrative poems, 'The Lady of the Lake', a romantic adventure involving a Scottish Highland Clan and set in the sixteenth century. Scott (1771–1832), trained as an Edinburgh lawyer, used his wide knowledge of Scottish Border and Highland history to produce, first, a highly successful series of long historical poems and, then, a succession of even more popular historical novels, most of them set in Scotland.

Scott's writing, both verse and prose, helped to popularise the Border Country and the Highlands of Scotland throughout Britain and Europe. It encouraged tourists, who had been influenced by the growing enthusiasm of artists, musicians and writers for dramatic mountain scenery in the late eighteenth and early nineteenth centuries, to visit the Scottish Highlands in ever-increasing numbers. Scott was, therefore, writing the sort of evocative verse and prose that his reading public relished, and one's view of this passage needs to take this into account; it aims to evoke a romantic impression for romantic readers.

In what ways do the ideal ingredients to appeal to the romantic spirit of Scott's readers already exist in the landscapes, the people, and the event presented here before Scott gets to work with his own romantic colouring? How does Scott enhance the romantic potential of the situation through the medium of his verse? What aspects of this view of Scotland would still appeal to visitors today? Although the romantic view of Scotland is good for the tourist trade how does it tend to distort the reality of life for the Highlanders both now and in the past? (Consider this poem alongside 'Glenaradale' (p. 69) and 'At the Highland Games'.)

At the Highland Games

A traditional feature of the activities at Highland Games has been the bagpiping competitions. The classical musical form of the bag-piper can be found in the pibroch, a series of variations for the bagpipe, chiefly martial but also including dirges commemorating fallen heroes. In this poem Iain Crichton Smith's reflections stem from his observing the performance of a piper at a Highland Games in the 1960s and from the stirring of the consciousness of his own ancestry evoked by the sounds of the pibroch.

What evidence does he present to support his opening image

in which he compares his savouring of a modern Highland Games with the re-reading of a book which has lost its pith – i.e. its spiritual *and* physical essence or strength? (Note his use of words which seem to suggest that one of the original qualities in the piper – that of coarse, masculine vitality – has been replaced by traits which seem almost effeminately dainty.) What do the references to 'crew-cuts' and 'cameras' suggest about one of the modern purposes of the Games?

'Finished. All of it's finished.' Try to analyse the qualities of national and racial pride which underly the despondency of this poem and the overall reasons for Iain Crichton Smith's despondency on this occasion.

Ancestors

This poem reflects the changes in remote parts of the Scottish coastline which took place in connection with the development of the North Sea oilfields during the 1970s. What particularly concerns the poet in connection with human depopulation and wild life in the remoter parts of Scotland at 'this back end of a century'? Why does he wish to 'tear my own life clear of these earlier lives where they yielded and were put to the sea', and why does he note that 'Their way too was of acceptance, ancestors'? Why does he voice the prayer that the wild should 'protect us from a stiffening of vision'? What does the word 'stiffening' seem to imply? What optimistic message does he perhaps see in his references to the wild creatures, and why is he 'leaving the wild to itself' in the last verse?

In what ways do the references to ancestry in this poem and in 'At the Highland Games' differ? How do the sentiments of 'Ancestors' differ from those of Walter Smith in 'Glenaradale' (p. 69)? Does 'Glenaradale' perhaps help to confirm Robin Munro's view about his ancestors' way of 'acceptance'?

From reading 'The Gathering', 'At the Highland Games' and 'Ancestors' what do you think these poems reveal of the contribution of the evocative qualities of the Scottish scenic and historical heritage to the fervour of Scottish national pride and, even, to the politics of nationalism?

Rome Remembered

Wet on the slate roofs and the yard awash;
No football for the day. I looked from my desk
At two cold boys lost on the Welsh tips,
Their hands fumbling, their frail knees
Scarred as mine from too many a
Reckless fall, the drill rain
Needling incessantly their dark pelts,
Their round, dark heads.

From what deep mouth of their need
The she-wolf came I do not remember.
The ripped sack of her coat,
Her narrow legs, her cautious feet asprawl,
There she was
In all the loud smell of her dampness.
She covered her foul teeth, her brute head bowed.
The wolf is a poor creature at best.

But they recognised her animal rescue,
Her warm dugs grey as coal, and lived.
They turned from a whimpering den to build
On any seven of our hills a mythical city.
Rome stands in the raw towers
Of fallen steel works, her eagle
Sails on the walls of sacked blast-furnaces,
Cinders cover her emperors.
Broken Remus is dead on the high moors.

Leslie Norris

The Gresford Disaster

You've heard of the Gresford disaster,
The terrible price that was paid;
Two hundred and forty-two soldiers were lost
And three men of a rescue brigade.

It occurred in the month of September;
At three in the morning that pit
Was wracked by a violent explosion
In the Dennis where dust lay so thick.

The gas in the Dennis deep section
Was packed like snow in a drift,
And many a man had to leave the coal-face
Before he had worked out his shift.

A fortnight before the explosion
To the shot-firer, Tomlinson cried:
'If you fire that shot we'll be all blown to hell!'
And no one can say that he lied.

The fireman's reports they are missing,
The records of forty-two days,
The colliery manager had them destroyed
To cover his criminal ways.

Down there in the dark they are lying,
They died for nine shillings a day;
They've worked out their shift and it's now they must lie
In the darkness until Judgement Day.

The Lord Mayor of London's collecting
To help both the children and wives.
The owners have sent some white lilies
To pay for the colliers' lives.

Farewell our dear wives and our children,
Farewell our dear comrades as well.
Don't send your sons in the dark dreary mine
They'll be damned like the sinners in Hell.

Anon

A Small War

Climbing from Merthyr through the dew of August mornings
When I was a centaur-cyclist, on the skills of wheels
I'd loop past The Storey Arms, past steaming lorries
Stopped for flasks of early tea, and fall into Breconshire.
A thin road under black Fan Frynych – which keeps its winter
Shillings long through spring – took me to the Senni valley.

That was my plenty, to rest on the narrow saddle
Looking down on the farms, letting the simple noises
Come singly up. It was there I saw a ring-ousel
Wearing the white gash of his mountains; but every
Sparrow's feather in that valley was rare, golden,
Perfect. It was an Eden fourteen miles from home.

Evan Drew, my second cousin, lived there. A long, slow man
With a brown gaze I remember him. From a hill farm
Somewhere on the slope above Heol Senni he sent his sons,
Boys a little older than I, to the Second World War.
They rode their ponies to the station, they waved
Goodbye, they circled the spitting sky above Europe.

I would not fight for Wales, the great battle-cries
Do not arouse me. I keep short boundaries holy,
Those my eyes have recognised and my heart has known
As welcome. Nor would I fight for her language. I spend
My few pence of Welsh to amuse my friends, to comment
On the weather. They carry no thought that could be mine.

It's the small wars I understand. So now that forty
People lock their gates in Senni, keeping the water out
With frailest barriers of love and anger, I'd fight for them.
Five miles of land, enough small farms to make a heaven,
Are easily trapped on the drawing-board, a decision
Of the pen drowns all. Yes, the great towns need

The humming water, yes, I have taken my rods to other
Swimming valleys and happily fished above the vanished
Fields. I know the arguments. It is a handful of earth
I will not argue with, and the slow cattle swinging weightily
Home. When I open the taps in my English bathroom
I am surprised they do not run with Breconshire blood.

Leslie Norris

NOTES

Rome Remembered

The industrial towns at the 'heads of the valleys' in South Wales owed their expansion to the development of the coal and iron industries in the nineteenth century. In the twentieth century came recession and unemployment, but the coal 'tips' and the abandoned works sites remained as symbols of past prosperity just as the ruins of Rome remain as symbols of the foundation of Rome by the legendary Romulus. This poem was written in the 1960s. In the 1980s the stark image of 'the raw towers of fallen steelworks' seems doubly and grimly apt since the closure of the steel works at Ebbw Vale, a works opened as recently as 1938 as part of government policy to aid the depressed areas in the recession of the 1930s.

Some of the images in this poem pose interesting questions. Why refer to the 'dark pelts' of the 'two cold boys' and why refer to the wolf's coat as 'the ripped sack'? Is there any special significance in imagining the wolf's dugs as being 'grey as coal'? Why are the blast-furnaces described as 'sacked'? In the legend the twins Romulus and Remus were suckled and saved from death by a she-wolf. Remus was killed by his brother after ridiculing the foundations of Rome laid by Romulus. What bearing does this have on the Welsh parallels in this poem? Why do 'cinders cover her emperors' and why is 'broken Remus .... dead on the high moors'?

At first sight the link between the poet's observing 'two cold boys lost on the Welsh tips' and the legend of the founding of Rome may appear merely fanciful. How does Leslie Norris convince his readers that the parallel he develops is symbolically valid?

The Gresford Disaster

The explosion at Gresford colliery in 1934 was one of the worst mining disasters of the century. The village of Gresford lies on the fringes of the small coalfield of North East Wales, close to the English border.

The very simple verse structure and rhythms of this narrative poem make it apt to be performed also as a folk song. At the same time this simplicity of structure tends to act as a control to a narrative which was clearly written with considerable personal feeling. As with newspaper reports of a disaster, the key fact concerning the great loss of life is stated in the opening verse; precise numbers are given. In what ways does the writer's concern throughout for precise figures add to the dramatic effect of the poem? What ironies and innuendoes lie within this narrative and how does the style of the poem underline these? How do the first and last verses establish a direct intimacy with the reader? To what audience is the writer addressing himself? What are the social undertones of the poem and how are they revealed? Why has this type of unsophisticated verse – read, spoken aloud or sung – become an accepted vehicle for expressions of social protest?

A Small War

The poet and short-story writer Leslie Norris was born and grew up around Merthyr Tydfil, an old iron industry town in the 'heads of the valleys' area of industrial South Wales, set in a landscape which probably provided the background for the poem 'Rome Remembered'. It is an area where the Welsh language is less used as the first language than in large areas in West, Central and North Wales – hence the reference, here, to 'my few pence of Welsh'. On the other hand, feelings about such matters as that referred to in this poem, the flooding of a Welsh valley and the loss of farms and farmland to provide water for towns, especially English towns, run, naturally, strongly.

Why does the construction of this poem (especially the use of the third verse as a bridge leading to the main theme of the poem) help to involve the reader more readily and intimately in the 'small war'? How do Leslie Norris's personal recollections of the Senni valley help you to identify with the plight of those whose homes are drowned by 'a decision of the pen'? In what ways is the personal style of the poem and the degree of personal involvement different from that of Leslie Norris's poem 'Rome Remembered'? What similarities are there in the sources of inspiration for both poems and the motivations behind them?

How does 'A Small War' differ from 'The Gresford Disaster' in the tone and the extent of its social protest? Does it share any common ground with 'The Gresford Disaster', a consciousness of exploitation perhaps?

An Ulster Garland

Close by my kitchen window juts
a wall, rich-textured, scarred
brickwork of ochre, grey and red
many times cemented, showing
faint whitewash from before
the house was last patched up.
And where the roof of split slates slopes
to its corner has somehow taken
root among fissures, a sprig
of wallflowers, arching
luminous now in the late sunshine.

Delicate, the flowers
have survived nights, and many downpours,
found sustenance amid crumbling.
I have come to expect them.

No, they would not, should it come,
prevail against bulldozer, or bomb;
nor admit their relevance.
And should these petals be torn by explosion,
buried deep under rubble, so
each unique thing must be lost, and is
irrevocable; yet always

others continue, reappear
contriving such root somewhere, so
configured on moving skies.

I drop my gaze on close
unfocused roofline ridges set
at jarring angles.

                    This
is Ireland now, where mobs command
and kill, and terror grips.
'The power system is at breakdown point.'

Lightless, I look
again for the yellow flowers upon
their brink; also remark
among the streets' cross-hatching sprays

of answering greenery, deepening
as day ebbs; in low
untended years, how cranesbill, vetch,
sweet rocket, speedwell, flowers
run wild I have no name for,
sustain their points of colour; and grass
persists, unorganized. By kind
pervasive to outlast
what coming darkness.

Andrew Waterman

Belfast

In the Phoenix Theatre where middle-class Celts
sipped Gaelic coffee from thick blue-glazed art-ware cups,
O'Casey's Juno keened again for Johnny dead
and the paycock rolled in his sodden surrender.

While in Divis Street another bird was rising
out of the ashes to cast a shadow of smoke
which, like a brown fog, appalled the city with what
could not be recalled now that it had been released.

In Donegall Place next day the young unemployed
gathered at bus-stops ignoring the buses but
waiting and smiling with no humour, expectant,
calling and laughing shortly,
like strings being tuned before a concert.

At the farm on the hillside, high above Belfast
we looked out and saw nothing but the grey-brown smoke,
that incense to an old god, which parted at times
to reveal small orange flames, soundless, like a dream.

Then later the sounds began that I could not place –
caught at last by the smell of Bonfire Night,
when I used to imagine a city besieged.
Although it's August, I'm cold.

Homeward, three small boys
dragging a new green park bench for a barricade;
new houses, unoccupied, all their windows smashed,
idle like the bus burned out in the Lower Falls.

Cars parked in the lane, their drivers, standing,
watch us as we turn away.
Fear, a suspicious dog stalking our heels,
growls and defies us to run.
We walk, with stiff backs.

Alan Hill, August 1969

Docker

There, in the corner, staring at his drink,
The cap juts like a gantry's crossbeam,
Cowling plated forehead and sledgehead jaw.
Speech is clamped in the lips' vice.

That fist would drop a hammer on a Catholic –
Oh yes, that kind of thing could start again;
The only Roman collar he tolerates
Smiles all round his sleek pint of porter.

Mosaic imperatives bang home like rivets;
God is a foreman with certain definite views
Who orders life in shifts of work and leisure.
A factory horn will blare the Resurrection.

He sits, strong and blunt as a Celtic cross,
Clearly used to silence and an armchair:
Tonight the wife and children will be quiet
At slammed door and smoker's cough in the hall.

Seamus Heaney

NOTES

An Ulster Garland

After reading through this poem what would you consider to be the purpose of its title? In what ways do the flowers which the writer observes around buildings and streets provide slender symbols of hope amidst the Northern Ireland troubles? Why do flowers lend themselves so aptly to such a wide variety of symbols in poetry? Note here, for instance, their paradox of being delicate but durable ('the flowers have survived nights' – what implications lie in the unqualified word 'nights'?), their power to lighten darkness and their power to provide spiritual light to outshine spiritual darkness.

'The power system is at breakdown point.' What is the effect of the intrusion of this prosaic, official-sounding statement at this stage in the poem? What are the implications of the word 'light-less' which follows the isolated three lines of reference to the violence and the political uncertainty in Ireland?

What special contribution can the poet make to one's view of contemporary events when he presents his personal view of those events? (This question is particularly relevant to one's considera-tion of 'war poets'.)

Belfast

Like the Phoenix, the legendary bird which, after burning itself to ashes on a funeral pyre, emerged from the ashes, with renewed youth, the IRA who, during the 1920s had fought a civil war against the British prior to the establishment of the Irish Free State and the British retention of the six counties of Ulster, emerged in the late 1960s in Belfast to renew the civil war in a campaign aimed ultimately at the establishment of a united Ire-land and the breaking of Ulster's links with Britain.

The performance of Irish playwright Sean O'Casey's play *Juno and the Paycock* at Belfast's Phoenix Theatre possesses a special significance when one bears in mind that the play is concerned with the Dublin 'troubles' of the 1920s. Juno is married to a feck-less, work-shy husband, 'Captain' Boyle who, nevertheless, enjoys 'Struttin' about the town like a paycock' (peacock). At the end of the play, after the Boyles' son Jimmy, an ardent Republican sus-pected of causing the death of a fellow IRA man, has been shot by the IRA, the 'paycock' returns home hopelessly drunk, unaware of

the murder, and capable only of observing that 'th' whole world's
...in a terr...ible...state of...chassis!' (chaos).

Tragic Art becomes here not just a reflection of life's tragedy
in the 1920s but a symbol of its resurgence in the 1960s. Do you
get the impression from Alan Hill's poem that the 'middle class
Celts' regarded the play in this way or as a cultural evening out?
How does Alan Hill establish in his poem the disturbing parallels
between art and life and also the impression that in August 1969
the symbolic phoenix was rising with renewed youth? What visual
resemblances to the phoenix legend does the poet explore in his
observations?

Docker

This poem was written before the escalation of the violence in
Northern Ireland in the late 1960s, hence the statement 'that kind
of thing could start again' in the second verse. What impressions
of the docker's physique, character and narrowness of domestic and
spiritual vision emerge from the poet's use of images drawn from
the shipyard to describe him? How do word *sounds* in this poem
contribute to the total impression conveyed of the docker? What
tensions are added to the poem by the references to the divisions
in the Christian church and by the manner of reference?

The Midlands

Black in the summer night my Cotswold hill
    Aslant my window sleeps, beneath a sky
Deep as the bedded violets that fill
    March woods with dusky passion. As I lie
Abed between cool walls I watch the host
    Of the slow stars lit over Gloucester plain,
And drowsily the habit of these most
    Beloved of English lands moves in my brain,
While silence holds dominion of the dark,
Save when the foxes from the spinneys bark.

I see the valleys in their morning mist
    Wreathed under limpid hills in moving light,
Happy with many a yeoman melodist:
    I see the little roads of twinkling white
Busy with field-ward teams and market gear
    Of rosy men, cloth-gaitered, who can tell
The many-minded changes of the year,
    Who know why crops and kine[1] fare ill or well;
I see the sun persuade the mist away,
Till town and stead are shining to the day.

I see the wagons move along the rows
    Of ripe and summer-breathing clover-flower,
I see the lissom husbandman who knows
    Deep in his heart the beauty of his power,
As, lithely pitched, the full-heaped fork bids on
    The harvest home. I hear the rickyard fill
With gossip as in generations gone,
    While wagon follows wagon from the hill.
I think how, when our seasons all are sealed,
Shall come the unchanging harvest from the field.

I see the barns and comely manors planned
    By men who somehow moved in comely thought,
Who, with a simple shippon[2] to their hand,
    As men upon some godlike business wrought;
I see the little cottages that keep
    Their beauty still where since Plantagenet
Have come the shepherds happily to sleep,
    Finding the loaves and cups of cider set;
I see the twisted shepherds, brown and old,
Driving at dusk their glimmering sheep to fold.

And now the valleys that upon the sun
    Broke from their opal veils are veiled again,
And the last light upon the wolds is done,
    And silence falls on flocks and fields and men;
And black upon the night I watch my hill,
    And the stars shine, and there an owly wing
Brushes the night, and all again is still,
    And, from this land of worship that I sing,
I turn to sleep, content that from my sires
I draw the blood of England's midmost shires.

John Drinkwater

[1] cows

[2] cowshed

You That Love England

You that love England, who have an ear for her music,
The slow movement of clouds in benediction,
Clear arias of light thrilling over her uplands,
Over the chords of summer sustained peacefully;
Ceaseless the leaves' counterpoint in a west wind lively,
Blossom and river rippling loveliest allegro,
And the storms of wood strings brass at year's finale:
Listen. Can you not hear the entrance of a new theme?

You who go out alone, on tandem or on pillion,
Down arterial roads riding in April,
Or sad beside lakes where hill-slopes are reflected
Making fires of leaves, your high hopes fallen:
Cyclists and hikers in company, day excursionists,
Refugees from cursed towns and devastated areas,
Know you seek a new world, a saviour to establish
Long-lost kinship and restore the blood's fulfilment.

You who like peace, good sticks, happy in a small way
Watching birds or playing cricket with schoolboys,
Who pay for drinks all round, whom disaster chose not;
Yet passing derelict mills and barns roof-rent
Where despair has burnt itself out – hearts at a standstill,
Who suffer loss, aware of lowered vitality;
We can tell you a secret, offer a tonic; only
Submit to the visiting angel, the strange new healer.

You above all who have come to the far end, victims
Of a run-down machine, who can bear it no longer;
Whether in easy chairs chafing at impotence
Or against hunger, bullies and spies preserving
The nerve for action, the spark of indignation –
Need fight in the dark no more, you know your enemies.
You shall be leaders when zero hour is signalled,
Wielders of power and welders of a new world.

Cecil Day Lewis

Watching Post

A hill flank overlooking the Axe valley.
Among the stubble a farmer and I keep watch
For whatever may come to injure our countryside –
Light-signals, parachutes, bombs, or sea-invaders.
The moon looks over the hill's shoulder, and hope
Mans the old ramparts of an English night.

In a house down there was Marlborough born. One night
Monmouth marched to his ruin out of that valley.
Beneath our castled hill, where Britons kept watch,
Is a church where the Drakes, old lords of this countryside,
Sleep under their painted effigies. No invaders
Can dispute their legacy of toughness and hope.

Two counties away, over Bristol, the searchlights hope
To find what danger is in the air tonight.
Presently gunfire from Portland reaches our valley
Tapping like an ill-hung door in a draught. My watch
Says nearly twelve. All over the countryside
Moon-dazzled men are peering out for invaders.

The farmer and I talk for a while of invaders:
But soon we turn to crops – the annual hope,
Making of cider, prizes for ewes. Tonight
How many hearts along this war-mazed valley
Dream of a day when at peace they may work and watch
The small sufficient wonders of the countryside.

Image or fact, we both in the countryside
Have found our natural law, and until invaders
Come will answer its need: for both of us, hope
Means a harvest from small beginnings, who this night
While the moon sorts out into shadow and shape our valley,
A farmer and a poet, are keeping watch.

Cecil Day Lewis, July 1940

NOTES

The Midlands

John Drinkwater was one of the so-called 'Georgian poets' (it was the reign of George V), a founder-member of a group who, between 1912 and 1922, published a number of anthologies of 'Georgian' poetry designed for the general reader who enjoyed reading poetry which was direct and simple in thought, 'beautiful' in expression, and strong in emotional appeal. The First World War (1914–18) produced a strong upsurge of patriotism and its horrors helped to popularise one type of 'Georgian' poem in particular – the poem which took for its theme the English countryside – country crafts, country folk, country life, country homes and scenes. This type of poem, not surprisingly, retained its popular appeal throughout the 1920s and into the 1930s. It provided a comfortable view of an apparently contented continuity of rural life in England, a sense of stability in a period of social and economic uncertainty. It may not have been an accurate reflection of country life and of attitudes amongst farm labourers (*did* the 'lissom husbandman' know 'deep in his heart the beauty of his power'?) but it provided consolation to many readers – particularly amongst the middle and upper classes – who liked to believe that it did.

Bearing in mind the period in which it was written and the public for which it was written, what effects would *then* have been created, do you think, by the extensive use of poetic diction in the poem? What qualities in the appearance, movement, behaviour and attitudes of the country people does the poet emphasise, and what impressions is he trying to create by doing so? In what ways would the effect of this poem on the readers for whom it was written be strengthened by John Drinkwater's deliberate use of emotive words and phrases and emotive expressions?

You That Love England

Reading the first verse of this poem one might at first think that Cecil Day Lewis is content with a variation of the theme explored in John Drinkwater's 'The Midlands' – until Day Lewis heralds 'the entrance of a new theme'.

Cecil Day Lewis was a member of a group of poets who began writing in the late 1920s and whose intentions were very different from John Drinkwater and his fellow 'Georgians'. This group included the poets W. H. Auden and Stephen Spender. All started writing in the years following the General Strike of 1926 and they matured against the background of the economic crash of 1929, the mass unemployment of the 1930s, the accession of Hitler to power in Germany in 1933, and the growing threats of Fascism, Communism and a new European War.

Many of their poems were idealistic calls for action, sometimes reflecting the left-wing sympathies typical of many intellectuals at the time.

In what ways is the use of musical terms in the first verse of the poem appropriate to the description of the English scene and how does the sustained musical metaphor provide the link with the following verses? To what sections of the population is Day Lewis specifically appealing in each of the verses? What seem to be the special implications of the address 'You *above all*' in the opening line of the last verse? How does the language of the second, third, and fourth verses reflect the social effects of this period of economic depression?

In view of Day Lewis's sympathies with Communism at that time, what might he be implying in the advice he gives to 'You above all . . .' in the final three lines of the poem?

In the 1930s Britain seemed to lack strong political leadership at the very time when the Fascist dictatorships of Hitler in Germany and Mussolini in Italy were becoming increasingly powerful and threatening. How is this reflected both in the emotive expressions used in the closing statements of each verse (words such as 'saviour' and 'visiting angel', for example) and in the very vagueness of what Day Lewis has to offer ('long-lost kinship', 'the blood's fulfilment')? In what ways does this poem perhaps reflect the difficulties facing poets who sought to use their art to reveal a positive sense of political commitment in the 1930s?

Watching Post

This poem was written in 1940 when there was a very real possibility that the Germans would invade southern England and when the Home Guard and other volunteers kept constant watch in southern counties.

In what ways does the mood and tone of this poem differ from the mood and tone of 'You That Love England', which was written only a few years previously? What is the relevance of the local historical associations to Day Lewis's thoughts and feelings in the poem? How might one account for the conservatism of this poem and its feeling for heritage and tradition when one compares it with the revolutionary mood of 'You That Love England'? What is the relevance of the poet's conversation with the farmer about crops to the thoughts of the last verse which link the farmer and the poet? (It is worth discussing the various symbolic uses of the images of 'crops' and 'harvest' frequently encountered in reflective poems.)

Are there *any* similarities, do you feel, between this poem and John Drinkwater's poem 'The Midlands'?

Admonition

Intended more particularly for the perusal of those who may have happened to be enamoured of some beautiful place of Retreat, in the Country of the Lakes.

Well may'st thou halt – and gaze with brightening eye!
The lovely Cottage in the guardian nook
Hath stirred thee deeply; with its own dear brook,
Its own small pasture, almost its own sky!
But covet not the Abode; – forbear to sigh,
As many do, repining while they look;
Intruders – who would tear from Nature's book
This precious leaf, with harsh impiety.
Think what the Home must be if it were thine,
Even thine, though few thy wants! – Roof, window, door,
The very flowers are sacred to the Poor,
The roses to the porch which they entwine:
Yes, all that now enchants thee, from day
On which it should be touched, would melt away.

William Wordsworth

A Summer Place

You know that house she called home,
so sleek, so clapboard-white, that
used to be some country jobber's blight
or scab on our hill's arm.
You can see the two cellars of the barn,
stones still squatting where the fellow stacked them.

He worked the place as a farm,
though how, with stones for soil, she never knew.
Partly she hoped he'd been a poet too –
why else hang Haystack mountain and its view
from north-west windows?
It was the view she bought it for. He'd gone.
The house sagged on its frame. The barns were down.

The use she saw for it was not to be
of use. A summer place. A lovely
setting where fine minds could graze
at leisure on long summer days
and gather books from bushes, phrase by phrase.
Work would be thought. A tractor bought for play
would scare unnecessary, ugly scrub away.

A white gem set on a green silk glove
she bought and owned there.
And summers wore it, just as she would wear
each summer like a dress of sacred air
until the house was half compounded of
foundations, beams and paint, half of her love.

She lived profoundly, felt, wrote from her heart,
knew each confessional songbird by its voice,
cloistered her garden with bee balm and fanning iris,
sat, stained by sunsets, in a vault of noise
listening through cricket prayer for whitethroat,
hermit thrush . . . and couldn't keep it out,
the shade of something wrong, a fear, a doubt.

as though she heard the house stir in its plaster,
stones depart unsteadily from walls,
the woods, unwatched, stretch out its roots like claws
and tear through careful fences, fiercer than saws.
Something alive lived under her mind-cropped pasture,
hated the house, or worse, loved, hungering after
its perfectly closed compactness, breathed disaster.

She dreamed or daydreamed what it might have come to,
with the house itself wanting the view
to take it, and the view's love gathering into
brambles, tendrils, trunks of maples, needing
her every window, entering, seeding.
Fear of imminent attack kept her from sleeping,
kept her awake in her white room, pacing, weeping.

But you see the place still stands there, pretty as new.
Whatever she thought the mountain and trees would do,
they did – and took her with them – and withdrew.

Anne Stevenson

96

NOTES

Admonition

This sonnet was first published in 1807. Wordsworth had returned to his native Lake District in December 1799 to settle at Dove Cottage, Grasmere, with his sister Dorothy, and he had married a friend of his childhood, Mary Hutchinson, in 1802.

Were he alive today, Wordsworth would, without doubt, be an ardent conservationist who would have plenty to say about townspeople buying up country cottages for retirement or for holiday homes in the major scenic areas of Britain, a practice which has resulted in prices soaring beyond the reach of local would-be purchasers. In this sonnet Wordsworth refers to those who would like the cottage purely as a 'beautiful place of retreat' as 'intruders'. Why does he regard them as 'intruders'? What does he see as being the real role of the Lakeland cottage and how does he depict the cottage as being a subtly integrated part of the natural environment? What precisely does he mean when he suggests that 'all that now enchants thee, from the day on which it should be touched, would melt away'?

That this poem was not just a whimsical outburst is clear if one reads Wordsworth's fascinating and provocative prose *Guide to the Lakes*, which is still in print and which remains highly relevant in its material. In the Guide he was highly critical of the incongruity of new buildings erected in the Lake District in the early nineteenth century. In contrast, he wrote, the older Lakeland cottages were integrated features of the landscape: 'these humble dwellings remind the contemplative spectator of a production of Nature, and may (using a strong expression) rather be said to have grown than to have been erected; – to have risen, by an instinct of their own, out of the native rock – so little is there in them of formality, such is their wildness and beauty.'

A Summer Place

After reading 'Admonition' one has the uneasy feeling that this poem tells the story of someone who failed to heed the admonition:

> Intruders – who would tear from Nature's book
> This precious leaf, with harsh impiety.

Reading 'A Summer Place' helps one to understand more precisely what Wordsworth was getting at, especially if one first considers the statement 'The use she saw for it was not to be of use. A summer place. A lovely setting...'

There was nothing of the insensitive townee sporting a holiday cottage in the occupant of this summer place. She was sensitive to her mountain surroundings; 'she lived profoundly, felt, wrote from her heart'. In harmony with nature, or so it seemed. Yet, 'It was the view she bought it for', and through her concern for its aesthetic rather than its utilitarian value she misjudged the building's original and essential function, that of a Lakeland farm, a building integrated with its environment.

Wordsworth, in his *Guide to The Lakes*, referred to the way in which 'the coverings and sides of the houses have furnished places of rest for the seeds of lichens, mosses, ferns, and flowers. Hence, buildings, which in their very form call to mind the processes of Nature, do thus, clothed in part with a vegetable garb, appear to be received into the bosom of the living principle of things, as it acts and exists among the woods and fields...'

Bearing in mind these comments of Wordsworth, how would you interpret the reference to 'the house itself wanting the view to take it...' in the penultimate verse of this poem? (Note the special implication of 'take' here.) What seemed wrong with the woman's treatment of the house and her surroundings, which is hinted at, for instance, in the opening two lines of the poem, and, especially, perhaps, the words 'so sleek'? Can houses seem to have living personalities? How is the house in this poem given a living personality and what effect does this have on the atmosphere and the seriousness of the poem? To what extent is the situation explored in the poem a credible interpretation of the problems of individuals seeking to settle into an environment which is alien to them?

Summer

The sky above the street is a bewildering
Blue, and lower between the rooftop
Chimneys it is still blue, a dazzling
Emptiness. The roadway sponges
As the tar melts and its smell comes up.

Every door hangs open on its hinges
Inviting air in, but the brickwork
Throws off a thick wad of warmth that punches
Through over the doorsteps. Parked cars
Sting the touch, glitter and make the eyeballs ache.

On the pavement between two doors,
Rugs spread on the hot slabs, two girls
Sit and murmur in snatches, neighbours
More neighbourly in companionable weather,
Gracefully sensuous, swapping lazy smiles.

One leans on an elbow, legs together
Flat, the divan pose of one who is looked at.
In a backless sundress the other
Arches to the road a vulnerable spine
Nubbling the sheet-smooth skin, bleached winter-white.

They have a conscious indolence, a beach-scene
Bravado under the windowsills. A bus
Drumming past feet away carries the routine
They are well out of, now. They glance slyly
At passengers pink and steaming behind glass.

John Cassidy

View From a Back Window

Bay State Road, Boston

A strip of street where nobody walks,
Cars, between dustbins, illegally park
('Police take notice'), fenced for safety
With concrete, wire, against the two-way flow
Of traffic on the throughway. Then,
Unfenced, the grassy bank, with trees, a path
Where nobody walks but joggers run.
Still closer to the wide dividing waters
That hardly seem to flow, their surface ripple
Flattened, slowed down by trucks, a bench more green
Than the short grass it stands on. There
A man – voyeur of beer cans, eavesdropper
On engine rumble, chassis rattle, screech
Of tyres, gratuitous inhaler
Of gases not his property – could sit
And, willing, strong enough to raise his eyes,
On the far bank observe the two-way flow
Of traffic on the throughway; then
The tall façades, bare tenement, turret of chateau,
Factory chimney, mosque rotunda, where
Behind the blocked view seeing could begin.

Michael Hamburger

NOTES

Summer

What, perhaps, are the conventional expectations of the reader encountering a poem entitled 'Summer' in a poetry anthology, and what, thus, gives the title of this poem a special relevance to John Cassidy's portrait? How does he communicate the feel of the atmosphere of a residential street typical of over-crowded inner-city areas on a hot summer afternoon? What does his portrait reveal of the adaptability of the two girls to the restrictions of their environment? What point is made by the reference to the passing bus? Does the poem contain any message – intended, implied or unconsciously present?

View From a Back Window

'Summer' looks at a street front. Is there any special significance in the title of *this* poem? Why, in comparison with 'Summer', does this town environment appear immediately hostile and depressing? How does Michael Hamburger, by a process of selection and juxtaposition of detail, underline the hostile and depressing nature of this environment? What effects are created by the focusing on what a man – 'voyeur of beer cans, eavesdropper on engine rumble' *could* sit and observe? In what ways does the presence of this one imagined watcher produce a totally different atmosphere from that produced by the *actual* presence of the two girls in 'Summer'? What is the message, certainly implied and probably intended, of Michael Hamburger's poem? What is implied by the relentless detailing of 'the blocked view' behind which 'seeing could begin' in the final lines of the poem?

On the Projected Kendal and Windermere Railway

Is then no nook of English ground secure
From rash assault?[1] Schemes of retirement sown
In youth, and 'mid the busy world kept pure
As when their earliest flowers of hope were blown,
Must perish; how can they this blight endure?
And must he too the ruthless change bemoan
Who scorns a false utilitarian lure
'Mid his paternal fields at random thrown?
Baffle the threat, bright Scene, from Orrest-head[2]
Given to the pausing traveller's rapturous glance:
Plead for thy peace, thou beautiful romance
Of nature; and, if human hearts be dead,
Speak, passing winds; ye torrents, with your strong
And constant voice, protest against wrong.

William Wordsworth

[1] *The degree and kind of attachment which many of the yeomanry feel to their small inheritances can scarcely be over-rated. Near the house of one of them stands a magnificent tree, which a neighbour of the owner advised him to fell for profit's sake. 'Fell it!' exclaimed the yeoman, 'I had rather fall on my knees and worship it.' It happens, I believe, that the intended railway would pass through this little property, and I hope that an apology for the answer will not be thought necessary by one who enters into the strength of the feeling.* (Wordsworth's Note)

[2] a popular view-point overlooking Windermere, in the Lake District.

The Town Clerk's Views

'Yes, the Town Clerk will see you.' In I went.
He was, like all Town Clerks, from north of Trent;
A man with bye-laws busy in his head
Whose Mayor and Council followed where he led.
His most capacious brain will make us cower,
His only weakness is a lust for power –
And that is not a weakness, people think,
When unaccompanied by bribes or drink.
So let us hear this cool careerist tell
His plans to turn our country into hell.
'I cannot say how shock'd I am to see
The *variations* in our scenery.

Just take for instance, at a casual glance,
Our muddled coastline opposite to France:
Dickensian houses by the Channel tides
With old hipp'd roofs and weather-boarded sides.
I blush to think one corner of our isle
Lacks concrete villas in the modern style.
Straight lines of hops in pale brown earth of Kent,
Yeomen's square houses once, no doubt, content
With willow-bordered horse-pond, oast-house, shed,
Wide orchard, garden walls of browny-red –
All useless now, but what fine sites they'ld be
For workers' flats and some light industry.
Those lumpy church towers, unadorned with spires,
And wavy roofs that burn like smouldering fires
In sharp spring sunlight over ashen flint
Are out of date as some old aquatint.
Then glance below the line of Sussex downs
To stucco terraces of seaside towns
Turn'd into flats and residential clubs
Above the wind-slashed Corporation shrubs.
Such Georgian relics should by now, I feel,
Be all rebuilt in glass and polished steel.
Bournemouth is looking up. I'm glad to say
That modernistic there has come to stay.
I walk the asphalt paths of Branksome Chine
In resin-scented air like strong Greek wine
And dream of cliffs of flats along those heights,
Floodlit at night with green electric lights.
But as for Dorset's flint and Purbeck stone,
Its old thatched farms in dips of down alone –
It should be merged with Hants and made to be
A self-contained and plann'd community.
Like Flint and Rutland, it is much too small
And has no reason to exist at all.
Of Devon one can hardly say the same,
But 'South-West Area One's' a better name,
For those red sandstone cliffs that stain the sea
By mid-Victoria's Italy – Torquay.
And 'South-West Area Two' could well include
The whole of Cornwall from Land's End to Bude.
Need I retrace my steps through other shires?
Pinnacled Somerset? Northampton's spires?
Burford's broad High Street is descending still
Stone-roofed and golden-walled her elmy hill

To meet the river Windrush. What a shame
Her houses are not brick and all the same.
Oxford is growing up to date at last.
Cambridge, I fear, is living in the past.
She needs more factories, not useless things
Like that great chapel which they keep at King's.
As for remote East Anglia, he who searches
Finds only thatch and vast, redundant churches.
But that's the dark side. I can safely say
A beauteous England's really on the way.
Already our hotels are pretty good
For those who're fond of *very simple food* –
Cod and veg., free pepper, salt and mustard,
Followed by nice hard plums and lumpy custard,
A pint of bitter beer for one-and-four,
Then coffee in the lounge a shilling more.
In a few years this country will be looking
As uniform and tasty as its cooking.
Hamlets which fail to pass the planners' test
Will be demolished. We'll rebuild the rest
To look like Welwyn mixed with Middle West.
All fields we'll turn to sports grounds, lit at night
From concrete standards by fluorescent light:
And over all the land, instead of trees,
Clean poles and wire will whisper in the breeze.
We'll keep one ancient village just to show
What England once was like when times were slow –
Broadway for me. But here I know I must
Ask the opinion of our National Trust.
And ev'ry old cathedral that you enter
By then will be an Area Culture Centre.
Instead of nonsense about Death and Heaven
Lectures on civic duty will be given;
Eurhythmic classes dancing round the spire,
And economics courses in the choir.
So don't encourage tourists. Stay your hand
Until we've really got the country plann'd.'

John Betjeman

Festival Notebook

CLOSING SCENES of the Salisbury Festival:
Haydn and Mozart in St Edmund's Church,
A building soon to be deconsecrated
Because irrelevant to civic needs
And turned into a meaningful hotel.
Involuntarily the mind throws up
Fancies of Japanese, back from Stonehenge,
Quaffing keg bitter by the pulpit stair,
Swedes booking coach-tours in the chancel.

SALISBURY becomes a part of Area 5
In 1974, and so its mayor,
Whose office dates back to 1611
(The year of the King James Bible, actually),
Will soon be as irrelevant as the church,
But need not be turned into anything.

LATER THAT NIGHT, outside the City Hall,
Past the Cadena, Debenham's, Joyland,
Men of the 1st Bn. the Royal Scots
Perform the historic ceremony of Tattoo.
Plaids, Bonnets, flash of tenor-drummers' sticks,
The pipes, stir the blood unmeaningfully
Till 'Jesus Christ, Superstar' rings out
In the quick march, and relevance is restored.

Kingsley Amis

NOTES

On the Projected Kendal and Windermere Railway

In the 1830s and 1840s there was as much opposition to the routing of new railways as there often is to the routing of new motorways today. The compact nature of the sonnet makes it a convenient, if infrequently utilised, vehicle for political, religious or social protest, and this sonnet was written by Wordsworth in his seventies specifically for publication in *The Morning Post* in the late autumn of 1844. He followed it up by writing two essay-length letters to the Editor of *The Morning Post*, setting out the local objections to the proposed railway in great detail. These letters can be read as Appendices to Ernest de Selincourt's edition of Wordsworth's *Guide to The Lakes* (Oxford paperback); their sentiments have a familiar ring today when conservationists have to mount ever-increasing opposition to new projects threatening major areas of natural beauty:

> Go to a pantomime, a farce, or a puppet-show, if you want noisy pleasure...but may those who have given proof that they prefer other gratifications continue to be safe from the molestation of cheap trains pouring out their hundreds at a time along the margin of Windermere...

For trains, now read cars and coaches; the M6, albeit passing a dozen or so miles east of Windermere, has achieved for The Lakes what Wordsworth feared.

Examine Wordsworth's selection of natural details, his style (note his use of rhetorical questions), his use of emotive words ('rash assault', for instance) in order to heighten the emotional power of his protest in this sonnet.

The Town Clerk's Views

John Betjeman's poem was written in the late 1940s, at a time when there was much talk about post-war planning and when the first signs were emerging of the 'planners' who have since wreaked havoc with the rural and urban environments of Britain. Like many examples of social satire, there are lines which have dated. The poem was written during the days of food rationing when hotel menus and catering were the unfortunate butt of English humour and when cod and plums *did* appear in mass catering with rather monotonous regularity! Yet the poem is particularly worth looking at today because some of Betjeman's fears which lurked behind his sardonic study of this 'cool careerist's' 'plans to turn our country into hell' have turned out to be well-founded. At Bournemouth there really are now 'cliffs of flats along these heights' at various points between Boscombe and Poole. Local Government reorganisation in 1974 didn't quite merge Dorset with Hants, but Bournemouth, Hants, was taken into Dorset despite strong protests from local residents at the time. We haven't quite got 'South-West Area One', but we have now got new metropolitan areas which ride roughshod across old county traditions; what could be more soulless than the amalgamation of certain strongly individual Lancashire towns into 'Greater Manchester', for instance?

What else in this poem has proved disturbingly prophetic?

Most of this poem is cast in the form of a 'dramatic monologue' (Victorian poet Robert Browning was a master of the 'dramatic monologue' – see, for instance, his poem 'My Last Duchess') in which a character is allowed to speak his thoughts and thus to reveal significant aspects of his character and personality. What does the Town Clerk reveal of his character and of his ideals in this poem? Since the dramatic monologue is obviously subject to the careful editing and cutting of the writer, what, then, does it reveal of John Betjeman's views on planning and conservation? How does Betjeman manage to convey his *own* sensitivity to architectural and scenic beauty through the medium of the Town Clerk's words? Betjeman uses the simple rhyming couplet as a deliberate vehicle for his irony. Look at the many examples of how the forced juxtaposition of observations *within* couplets can create an ironic tone. What effects are created by the carefully heavy use of rhymes?

Festival Notebook

In 'The Town Clerk's Views' John Betjeman unknowingly anticipated Local Government reorganisation in his reference to 'South-West Area One'. By 1974 it had happened, and Kingsley Amis, in his poem, notes that 'Salisbury becomes a part of Area 5' and its ancient mayoral office becomes 'irrevelant'. How do the words 'irrelevant', 'meaningful', 'unmeaningfully' and 'relevance' produce ironic links between each of the three verses of this poem? The Salisbury Festival of Music and Arts is now an established event in that city and will no doubt continue to be so. What reflections on bureaucratic decision-making emerge from the references to local government changes in the context of the closing scenes of the Festival in this poem? What is the significance, to the poet, of the playing of 'Jesus Christ, Superstar' at the Tattoo, and of the playing of Haydn and Mozart in St Edmund's Church?

What does Kingsley Amis appear to see as the *bureaucratic* definition of the words 'relevant' and 'meaningful'? What aspects of his visit to Salisbury appear to be most disturbing to him?

The Unknown Citizen

(To JS/07/M/378 This Marble Monument is Erected by the State).

He was found by the Bureau of Statistics to be
One against whom there was no official complaint,
And all the reports on his conduct agree
That, in the modern sense of an old-fashioned word, he was a
      saint,
For in everything he did he served the Greater Community.
Except for the War till the day he retired
He worked in a factory and never got fired,
But satisfied his employers, Fudge Motors Inc.
Yet he wasn't a scab or odd in his views,
For his Union reports that he paid his dues,
(Our report on his Union shows it was sound)
And our Social Psychology workers found
That he was popular with his mates and liked a drink.
The Press are convinced that he bought a paper every day
And that his reactions to advertisements were normal in every
      way.
Policies taken out in his name prove that he was fully insured,
And his Health-card shows that he was once in hospital but left it
      cured.
Both Producers Research and High-Grade Living declare
He was fully sensible to the advantages of the Instalment Plan
And had everything necessary to the Modern Man,
A phonograph, a radio, a car and a frigidaire.
Our researchers into Public Opinion are content
That he held the proper opinions for the time of year;
When there was peace, he was for peace; when there was war, he
      went.
He was married and added five children to the population,
Which our Eugenist says was the right number for a parent of his
      generation,
And our teachers report that he never interfered with their
      education.
Was he free? Was he happy? The question is absurd:
Had anything been wrong, we should certainly have heard.

W. H. Auden

The Disinherited

I

Pity the small, the pale forked figure, Man –
Of all the creatures short on dignity,
Hairless, unfleet and no great piece of work:
Buttoned and zipped and shod, fed from neat packs,
Deodorized, sweatproofed and analysed –
Where can he go to touch the roots of life?

Flown above storm in pressurized machines
Or sped through landscapes, cushioned, warm and dry;
Painfree, alert or tranquillized through drugs,
He turns to sex or violence, bursting out
From the cold capsule, the safe envelope
That insulates him from the life of things.

Poor urban Man, the disinherited,
No longer born to loving enmity
With sea or soil, dead to the season's round,
He winces at the stark light science throws
And burrows back again towards the dark
The ever-living, fertile mysteries.

II

Faces stream past me, unidentified
As iron filings in a magnet's field.
Since no one knows me, can I know I'm here?
If I fell dead they would tread over me.
I will smash something, shout, disrupt, destroy
Then they will know and I will know I live.

III

Each is alone and lost. If we two strip
Flesh will find flesh and mouths will need no words.
We who are shorn of ceremony now
Can still perform this rite, oldest of all,
Enter the heart of darkness and make flower
The last instinctive blossom on the tree.

Joan Murray Simpson

Nocturne

Under the winter street-lamps, near the bus-stop,
Two people with nowhere to go fondle each other,
Writhe slowly in the entrance to a shop.
In the intervals of watching them, a sailor
Yaws about with an empty beer-flagon,
Looking for something good to smash it on.

Mere animals: on this the Watch Committee
And myself seem likely to agree;
But all this fumbling about, this wasteful
Voiding of sweat and breath – is that *animal*!

Nothing so sure and economical

These keep the image of another creature
In crippled versions, cocky, drab and stewed?
What beast holds off its paw to gesture,
Or gropes towards being understood?

Kingsley Amis

To an Independent Preacher

Who preached that we should be 'in harmony with Nature'.

'In harmony with Nature'? Restless fool,
Who with such heat dost preach what were to thee,
When true, the last impossibility;
To be like Nature strong, like Nature cool: –
Know, man hath all which Nature hath, but more,
And in that *more* lie all his hopes of good.
Nature is cruel; man is sick of blood:
Nature is stubborn; man would fain adore:
Nature is fickle; man hath need of rest:
Nature forgives no debt, and fears no grave:
Man would be mild, and with safe conscience blest.
Man must begin, know this, where Nature ends;
Nature and man can never be fast friends.
Fool, if thou canst not press her, rest her slave!

Matthew Arnold

NOTES

The Unknown Citizen

Like John Betjeman's poem 'The Town Clerk's Views' (p. 102), this poem has proved to be disturbingly prophetic. What are the implications of the title and the sub-title? What is suggested by the absence of named personalities from this poem? What has happened to individuals? Why has the State erected a monument to JS/07/M/378? (Study the expressions and words such as 'no official complaint', 'served', 'reactions...normal', 'fully sensible to...')

Auden emigrated to the United States from England in 1939 and later became an American citizen. Although this poem is directed at the processing of the individual into American capitalist society, it is now equally relevant to the position of the individual in Britain, particularly since the introduction of computer storage of personal details of individual lives. What parallels now exist between Auden's 'report' and some present-day practices? Is Auden suggesting here, perhaps, that the bureaucratic organisations within the capitalist state are as capable of removing individual freedom as those within the communist state? (What do you make of the remark, 'Our teachers report that he never interfered with their education,' for instance?) Under the guise of an official 'report', Auden presents his own critical views of social trends. How does he achieve this? (Consider the juxtaposition of details, the use of titles such as 'Producers Research', the ironic use of the style of official reports.)

Discuss the import of the last two lines of the poem. In what ways might we 'hear' that something *is* wrong today? (See the following poem, 'The Disinherited'.)

The Disinherited

'Had anything been wrong, we should certainly have heard' is the final statement in Auden's report on 'The Unknown Citizen'. In this poem Joan Murray Simpson suggests that man's turning to sex or violence is one result of his being constricted by the scientific control of modern living within 'the safe envelope that insulates him from the life of things'. What, in her eyes, makes man so uniquely vulnerable to becoming detached from 'the roots of life'and how does science aid this process? Why is 'urban Man' specially at risk? What is the special meaning of the word 'disinherited' here? What special relevance, perhaps, has the second section of this poem to the implications of Auden's 'The Unknown Citizen'? Does Joan Murray Simpson make a valid link between lack of identity and the urge to be destructive in thought and deed? To what extent do you agree with her suggestion in the final section that the sexual act can thus be regarded as a ritual return to the only instinctive act left to man?

Joan Murray Simpson regards man as 'no great piece of work' and it is interesting to note that the words 'piece of work' have been used before in a very different assessment of man given by Hamlet in Shakespeare's play:

> What a piece of work is a man, how noble in reason, how infinite in faculties, in form and moving how express and admirable in action, how like an angel in apprehension, how like a god: the beauty of the world; the paragon of animals ...

Does one's assessment of man thus depend on whether or not one admits his divine origin, as sixteenth century thought did?

Nocturne

In what ways is the attitude to sex in this poem different from that found in Joan Murray Simpson's 'The Disinherited'? Of what does Kingsley Amis particularly disapprove in the behaviour of the couple near the bus-stop? How does their behaviour and that of the sailor perhaps *confirm* the assessment of man given in the first three lines of 'The Disinherited'?

What range of evocative meaning lies in the title of this poem and how does it, perhaps, indicate an ironic approach to the observations contained within the poem?

To an Independent Preacher

The beliefs of a poet are partly conditioned by the age in which he or she lives. What are the differences in attitude to the relationship of man to nature between this poem and 'The Disinherited'? How much are these differences attributable to the fact that Matthew Arnold was writing from a nineteenth century viewpoint and Joan Murray Simpson from a twentieth century viewpoint? For instance, in what ways, in the nineteenth century, was nature in the process of being tamed and harnessed by the scientific and mechanical inventions of man, and in what ways was man, in his colonisation and economic development of the wildernesses of, say, America, overcoming the 'cruel...stubborn...fickle' characteristics of nature? In this context, what is the meaning of the last line of Arnold's poem?

Is Arnold more easily able to draw these conclusions because of the Victorian belief in individual initiative and enterprise?

Jodrell Bank

Who were they, what lonely men
Imposed on the fact of night
The fiction of constellations
And made commensurable
The distances between
Themselves, their loves, and their doubt
Of governments and nations?
Who made the dark stable

When the light was not? Now
We receive the blind codes
Of spaces beyond the span
Of our myths, and a long dead star
May only echo how
There are no loves nor gods
Men can invent to explain
How lonely all men are.

Patric Dickinson

The Dark City

The lighted city is dark, but somewhere a bus
Glows and flares up in a hearth of coal-black space
And with its headlights singles out a face
Lost in a night of enormous loneliness.

Lost in the night of enormous loneliness
Which is his life, man looks for signs of light:
They are the small camp fires which put to flight
The beasts that prowl towards his helplessness.

The beasts that prowl towards our helplessness
Are brave in darkness, but in light they run
To deep subconscious caves in the mind of man
For whom a light is a home in homelessness.

Clifford Dyment

At a Memorial Service

All here are formalists.[1]
In the cruciform church
all stand facing east. All kneel.
Each muffles his faith, or no faith,
in old clean robes of prayer.
All attend, as words model
an image of a man they remember.
Here and there in a grey head
remembrance now stings
disused lachrymal ducts.

As a death brings them back to
their inherited cult
those decent grey heads,
respectful, respected,
conforming, are calmed.
One man less, they're estranged
that much more from the angry
menace outside,
the mad new Establishment
of loud disrespect.

As they rise to intone
an articulate hymn,
beneath it, in unison,
breathes a vast sighing
out of old tribal times:
migrant birds over oceans
rush, not knowing why,
their consensus of confidence
one soft brush touching
danger, day, and the dark.

William Plomer

[1] See the note for this poem p. 117.

NOTES

Jodrell Bank

An individual's belief in God provides an inner security, and this inner security is enhanced if the belief encompasses the concrete idea of a Heaven in the sky. Space exploration has robbed man of the latter idea and has thus, consciously or unconsciously, increased the private isolation of individual man.

What does Patric Dickinson see as the original purpose of the naming of the stars and of the stories associated with them? (It is worth considering not only the legends created around the various constellations but also the ways in which the stars and planets formed a part of mediaeval Christian belief in an ordered universe controlled by God in Heaven.) What does the poet now see as the effects of the knowledge of space gained from radio telescopes such as that at Jodrell Bank, Cheshire, on those who once found security in 'the fiction of constellations'?

The Dark City

Despite the stabilising and consoling qualities of an individual's religious beliefs, there yet exists a more primitive fear generated by the presence of the darkness of night.

How do Clifford Dyment's images in this poem link the origins of night fears of primitive man with the symbols of their continued existence within the mind of civilised man?

'Poor urban Man', remarked Joan Murray Simpson in her poem 'The Disinherited' (p. 109). Why does Clifford Dyment choose to illustrate the loneliness of individual man by setting his poem in 'The Dark *City*'?

At a Memorial Service

The first line of this poem contains an example of the apt range of meaning that can be concentrated within a single word. The Shorter Oxford Dictionary gives three definitions of the word 'formalist':

1 A solemn pretender to wisdom.
2 A time-server in religion.
3 A stickler for forms, etiquette, routine, or ceremonial.

How does William Plomer's use of the word contribute to his analysis of the older members of the congregation at a memorial service? (In what ways is the composition of a congregation at a memorial service very different from that at one of the regular services of the Church?) In the first verse, how does the image 'muffles . . . in old clean robes' actually clarify the role of prayer for the mourners? Is there a special purpose in Plomer's use of the word 'lachrymal' instead of the word 'tears' – bearing in mind the association of 'lachrymal' with mourning and with 'lachrymae Christi' (Christ's tears)?

What consolations does William Plomer seem to imply in the second verse exist for the elderly at a memorial service? What does the phrase 'inherited cult' suggest about the role of religion in the lives of occasional churchgoers?

What primitive implications emerge in the last verse in the assessment of the underlying reactions of the congregation to the hymn singing? In what ways do these implications link up with thoughts and images in Clifford Dyment's poem 'The Dark City', and, possibly, with thoughts in Patric Dickinson's 'Jodrell Bank'?

Primadonna

Age cannot wither her, for youth has done it;
But the vicissitudes of mortal progress
May yet transform a bitch into an ogress.

Observe without dismay the handsome face.
The yellow teeth and yellow conjunctiva,
The mouth agleam with lipstick and saliva

And marked with vices she has only dreamed,
Reveal a certain paralysing charm
Like that of the stone heads on Notre Dame.

On those above, and far enough below,
She turns a wet, ingratiating smile,
A voice to wheedle, flatter and beguile.

But read between the lines, the face is harsh;
The smile is but the mirror of a mind
By flagellation-fantasies refined.

Let but some near-subordinate rebel –
How quickly vanishes the obsequious leer
And the cajoling voice becomes a sneer.

It is her pride to call a spade a spade,
And when her spade bisects the offending worm,
It is her joy to see the pieces squirm.

Better be in the wrong than prove her wrong.
Then hear her bluster, bully, rage and fret,
And stamp and strut and play the martinet.

But let bad luck assail her, or self-doubt,
Then see the ego droop, the spirit sink,
Until restored by flattery or drink.

James Reeves

In Church

'And now to God the Father,' he ends,
And his voice thrills up to the topmost tiles:
Each listener chokes as he bows and bends,
And emotion pervades the crowded aisles.
Then the preacher glides to the vestry-door,
And shuts it, and thinks he is seen no more.

The door swings softly ajar meanwhile,
And a pupil of his in the Bible class,
Who adores him as one without gloss or guile,
Sees her idol stand with a satisfied smile
And re-enact at the vestry-glass
Each pulpit gesture in deft dumb-show
That had moved the congregation so.

Thomas Hardy

Leader of Men

When he addressed ten thousand
Faces worked by automation
He was filled, exalted, afflated
With love and ambition for
His fellowcountrymen – in so far,
Of course,
As they were not incompatible
With the love and ambition he felt
For himself. No sacrifice
Would be too great. No
Holocaust. No bloodbath. He
Was affected by the nobility
Of his vision, his eyes were,
Naturally, blurred.

How was he to know
The mindless face of the crowd
Broke up, when he finished, into
Ten thousand pieces – except that,
When he went home,
He found the tea cold, his wife
Plain, his dogs smelly?

Norman MacCaig

119

NOTES

Primadonna

A frequent source of humour in literature is the behaviour of public figures, particularly when their roles can easily expose them to caricature or to ridicule. The leading female singer in opera, the primadonna, has sometimes been vulnerable because of the legend that she can be temperamental and difficult to work with, and partly because, being employed for her singing ability rather than for her looks, an ageing, far from attractive singer tends to look somewhat incongruous when singing the role of a beautiful young heroine. It is only fair to say that there are many great operatic singers whose attractions befit the roles they sing!

The legendary stories of the operatic primadonnas have given rise to comparison of the behaviour of women in other walks of life with that of primadonnas, hence the expression 'behaving like a primadonna'. James Reeves, therefore, may not necessarily be confining his portrait to that of a singer.

The opening line of his poem begins with an intentional reference to the beauty and the sexual attractiveness of Cleopatra, described so sensuously by Enobarbus in Shakespeare's *Antony and Cleopatra*:

> Age cannot wither her, nor custom stale
> Her infinite variety: other women cloy
> The appetites they feed, but she makes hungry
> Where most she satisfies ...

How does James Reeves's deliberate misquotation establish the style and tone of his poem from the outset? What evidence of deliberate caricature is there in the poem? Why is the rhyming an important aspect of the tone and the total effect of the poem? Is James Reeves's portrait motivated by amusement, by a certain hostility, or by both? Of what does he appear to disapprove in his Primadonna?

In Church

Another public figure vulnerable to caricature is the local priest or vicar. 'In Church' is one of Thomas Hardy's short and pithy 'Satires of Circumstance'. In what ways does Hardy go about presenting an altogether more gentle portrait of the preacher than does James Reeves of the Primadonna?

Leader of Men

What is Norman MacCaig's purpose here in presenting the contrast between the public face and the private face of this 'leader of men'? What evidence is there that the speaker is an illusionist capable not merely of conning his listeners but also of conning himself? What evidence is there also to suggest that the speaker relies on a combination of visionary style and emotive language to create his effects? What does the whole poem suggest about the magnetism of a powerful speaker and about its dangers? What is suggested by the progressive intensity of the three words 'Filled, exalted, afflated' and by the sequence of negatives – 'No . . . no . . . no'?

Do the three poems – 'Primadonna', 'In Church' and 'Leader of Men' – suggest that egocentricity is a common and necessary characteristic of the three diverse characters portrayed?

The Magician

Off stage, the Great Illusionist owns bad teeth,
cheats at cards, beats his second wife, is lewd;
before studying his art he qualified
as obsessional liar, petty thief.

Transformed by glamorous paraphernalia –
tall top hat, made-up face, four smoking spotlights –
only fellow magicians can sense beneath
that glossy surface, a human failure.

Ready with unseen wires, luminous paint,
with drums and ceremony he fills the stage,
rich twice nightly in his full regalia.
Two extras planted in the audience faint.

Allezup! Closes his eyes, seemingly bored,
and astutely fakes a vulgar miracle,
mutters and reclines to become fakir, saint;
on a hotbed of nails, swallows a sword.

For encore will saw a seedy blonde in half
as music rises to a shrill crescendo;
hacks through wood, skin, vertebrae, spinal cord,
and all except the gods applaud or laugh.

Lord, red blood oozes from the long black box,
oh hocus pocus, oh abracadabra,
whilst, in trumped-up panic, manager and staff
race breathlessly on stage, undo the locks.

Patrons prefer bisected blondes to disappear.
Relieved, commercial men and their average wives
now salaciously prepare for further shocks,
eagerly yearn to see what they most fear.

Sometimes, something he cannot understand
happens – atavistic powers stray unleashed,
a raving voice he hardly thought to hear,
the ventriloquist's dummy out of hand.

In the box, a vision of himself – and on
those masochistic nails fresh genuine blood,
within his white glove a decomposing hand,
and, unimaginably, his own face gone.

Quite disturbed the disconnected audience boo.
What cheek! This charlatan believes his magic:
not luminous paint across the darkness shone
when happily, for once, his lies came true.

Or so it seemed. Oh what overbearing pride
if no longer fake but Great Illusionist;
But as phony critics pierce him through and through
he begs for mercy and is justified.

Off stage, that Great Illusionist owns bad teeth,
cheats at cards, beats his second wife, is lewd;
before studying his art he qualified
as obsessional liar, petty thief.

Dannie Abse

Grand Opera

The lovers have poisoned themselves and died singing,
And the crushed peasant father howls in vain.
For his duplicity, lubricity and greed
The unspeakable base count is horribly slain.

After the music, after the applause,
The lights go up, the final curtain drops.
The clerks troop from the house, and some are thinking:
Why is life different when the singing stops?

All that hysteria and histrionics,
All those coincidences were absurd,
But if there were no relevance to life,
Why were they moved to shudder and applaud?

Though they outlived that passion, it was theirs,
As was the jealousy, the sense of wrong
When some proud jack-in-office trampled them;
Only it did not goad them into song.

The accidents, the gross misunderstandings,
Paternal sorrow, amorous frustration
Have they not suffered? Was the melodrama
An altogether baseless imitation?

James Reeves

The Axe in the Orchard

In the summer of 1911, when Chekhov had been dead for seven years, The
Cherry Orchard *was first performed in London. It was afterwards re-
ported that at the end of the second act 'signs of disapproval were very
manifest indeed, and the exodus from the theatre began'. By the end of the
third act half the audience had departed.*

Nothing was heard but a whisper
Of satin. A notable couple
    Were shown to their places,
Well mated, assured, and upholding
An air of combined high command on
    Their thoroughbred faces.

Sir Something and Lady Someone
(No one remembers them now) –
    She, an Edwardian goddess
With a helmet of maid-brushed hair,
Pearls, and two velvet roses
    Blush-pink in her bodice,

To people she knew bowing slightly,
With the soldierly head of Sir Something
    More rigidly slanted,
His important moustache manifesting
Its wearer a person deferred to,
    Not taken for granted.

Oh, why were they there at the theatre?
They were idle, not curious; a hostess
    Ought to be able,
Lady Someone believed, to show up-to-dateness
And stimulate talk about plays among
    Guests at her table.

Between them and the stage loomed a spectral
Wave-ruling flagship, obscuring
    The sense of the show;
Sir Something and Lady Someone
Never guessed it was doomed and would founder,
    The ship *Status Quo*.

Sir Something's cold glare at his programme
Was like that he turned on from the Bench
    At some rustic offender;
Nothing was heard but his 'Well, now'
(Meaning 'Let's get it over'),
    'Let's see the agenda.'

'Who is this feller? A Russian?
Never heard of him, what? But I bet
    He can't hold a candle
To Arthur Pinero. God help us,
These damn foreign names! Four acts of it, too!
    I call it a scandal.'

Lady Someone said, 'Hush, dear, I know.' She
Was used to his testy complaining.
    Soon nothing was heard
But his mutter, 'Impossible people!
Dull twaddle! Nothing is *happening*!
    The whole thing's absurd!'

Disapproval can circulate quickly;
By the end of Act Two he declared it
    High time to go,
And they rose, with their vertical backbones,
To snub this *new* playwright they'd settled
    Was worthless to know.

But, as was ordained, when the actors
Had gone, when the stage was deserted,
    At the end of the play,
Nothing was heard but the strokes of
The axe in the orchard, the strokes
    of the axe far away.

The strokes of the axe in the orchard
Soon grew louder, unbearably thudding
 By night and by day;
Then nothing was heard but the guns in
The orchards of France. All at once Russia
 Was less far away.

William Plomer

NOTES

The Magician

As with the poem 'Leader of Men', one is made aware again here
of the contrast between the professionalism of the public man and
the seedy nature of the private man. What is the purpose of Dannie Abse's repetition of the opening verse at the end of the poem?
What is the significance of the magician's nightly transformation,
described in the second verse? How does Dannie Abse convey to
his readers the excitements of the magician's act in the theatre?

Dannie Abse is a doctor and his use of the word 'atavistic' is
interesting here; pathologically, the word refers to 'the power of
recurrence of the disease or constitutional symptoms of an ances-
tor after the intermission of one or more generations' (*Shorter Oxford English Dictionary*). Is he suggesting here that the Great Illusion which the magician himself occasionally experiences is a temporary belief in the effectiveness of his own magic which his *profes-
sional* ancestors in the remoteness of time possessed, a moment in
which his own act seems not fake but real?

Does this poem add any disturbing dimensions to the experience of stage magic?

Why, according to Dannie Abse, do the most disturbing parts
of the magician's act have a special appeal for some members of
the audience? Consider particularly the words 'eagerly yearn to
see what they most fear'.

Grand Opera

What comparisons can be made do you think, between the *underlying* appeal of the magician's act to the audience in Dannie Abse's
poem and the *underlying* appeal of the grand opera which moved
the clerks in the audience 'to *shudder* and applaud'? For what
reasons do some of the clerks ask themselves 'Why is life different
when the singing stops?'? What aspects of opera – 'hysteria and

histrionics', for instance – tend to obscure the relevance of grand opera plots to life? What 'relevance to life' does James Reeves find in this particular grand opera?

Why is opera a particularly appropriate medium for the illustration and exploration of human passions, and, especially, tragic passions? (Look at some of the plots of the most popular grand operas!)

The Axe in the Orchard

In what ways does the role of the audience in this poem differ from the role of the audience in the poems 'Grand Opera' and 'The Magician'? Why, in each poem, is the poet interested in both performance *and* audience?

What does this poem reveal of the social reasons for the presence of the aristocratic members of the 1911 audience? How does William Plomer establish the links between their lives of privilege and authority and the way in which they respond to a new play from a great Russian playwright with closed minds and boorish reactions? What is the significance of the image of the 'wave-ruling flagship...the ship *Status Quo*'? ('Status quo' means 'the existing state of things' and is an expression often used by people who wish to retain an existing way of life and who oppose change, social change in particular.)

'The strokes of the axe' are heard in the last moments of Chekhov's play; they herald the chopping down of the trees in the cherry orchard. The orchard has been sold, along with the rest of the estate of Mme Ranevsky, in order to pay her debts. Ironically, the English audience of 1911 was in fact watching a play concerned with the ending of the status quo for a Russian family. To the character Trofimov, a long-term university student, the family cherry orchard symbolises a couple of hundred years of lagging behind. In the Second Act of the play Trofimov observes: 'In order to start to live in the present, we must first of all redeem our past, have done with it, and its redemption can be achieved only through suffering, only through tremendous, incessant labour.' How prophetic would those words have eventually appeared to the audience of 1911 had they listened! What events is William Plomer referring to in the last verse of the poem?

Sir Something, in the poem, muttered 'Nothing is *happening!*' as he watched the play. He (but not William Plomer) probably missed the point of Mme Ranevsky's comment in Act Two: 'It is not plays you should go to look at, but look at yourselves a little more often. How grey your lives are!'

An Academic

How sad, they think, to see him homing nightly
In converse with himself across the quad,
Down by the river and the railway arch
To his gaunt villa and his squabbling brood,
His wife anchored beside a hill of mending.
Such banal evenings – how they pity him.

By day his food is Plato, Machiavelli,
'Thought is a flower, gentlemen,' he says –
Tracing the thought in air until it grows
Like frost-flowers on the windows of the mind –
'Thought is a flower that has its roots in dung.'
What irony, they think, that one so nourished,
Perfect in all the classic commonwealths,
Himself so signally should lack the arts
To shine and burgeon in the College councils,
A worn-out battery, a nobody, a windbag.
'And yet,' they sigh, 'what has the old boy got,
That every time he talks he fills the hall?'

James Reeves

The French Master

Everyone in Class II at the Grammar School
had heard of Walter Bird, known as Wazo.
They said he'd behead each dullard and fool
or, instead, carve off a tail for the fun.

Wazo's cane buzzed like a bee in the air.
Quietly, quietly, in the desks of Form III
sneaky Wazo tweaked our ears and our hair.
Walter Wazo, public enemy No. 1.

Five feet tall, he married sweet Doreen Wall
and combmarks furrowed his vaselined hair;
his hands still fluttered ridiculously small,
his eyes the colour of a poison bottle.

Who'd think he'd falter, poor love-sick Walter
as bored he read out *Lettres de mon Moulin*;
his mouth had begun to soften and alter,
and Class IV ribbed him as only boys can.

Perhaps through kissing his wife to a moan
had alone changed the shape of his lips,
till the habit of her mouth became his own:
no more Walter Wazo, enemy No. 1.

'Boy,' he'd whine, 'yes, please decline the verb to have,'
in tones dulcet and mild as a girl.
'Sorry sir, can't sir, must go to the lav,'
whilst Wazo stared out of this world.

Till one day in May Wazo buzzed like a bee
and stung, twice, many a warm, inky hand;
he stormed through the form, a catastrophe,
returned to this world, No. 1.

Alas, alas, to the Vth Form's disgrace
nobody could quote Villon to that villain.
Again the nasty old mouth zipped on his face,
and not a weak-bladdered boy in the class.

Was Doreen being kissed by a Mr Anon?
Years later, I purred, 'Your dear wife, Mr Bird?' –
Teeth bared, how he *glared* before stamping on;
and suddenly I felt sorry for the bastard.

Dannie Abse

'Here Comes Sir George'

The boys wink at the boys: 'Here comes Sir George.'
Yes, here he comes, punctual as nine o'clock
With bad jokes buzzing at his ramrod back –
'Victoria's Uncle', 'Rearguard of the Raj'.

They do not know or, if they know, forget
The old fool held a province down larger
Than England; not as a Maharaja
Prodigal with silver and bayonet;

But with cool sense, authority and charm
That still attend him, crossing a room
With the *Odes of Horace* under his arm
And in his button-hole a fresh-cut bloom.

Honour the rearguard, you half-men: for it
Was, in retreat, the post of honour. He –
Last of the titans – is worth your study.
You are not worth the unsheathing of his wit.

Jon Stallworthy

NOTES

An Academic

How is the isolated brilliancy of this public figure conveyed in the
poem? What does the single quotation from his lecture demonstrate? The word 'burgeon' means 'to shoot out or to put forth as
buds'. For what reasons does James Reeves use this word in relation to what are probably very prosaic discussions in the College
Councils? With whom do you think James Reeves is in sympathy,
the 'academic' or the members of the College Council – and why?
What is the shade of meaning suggested in the use of the word
'academic' in the title, and why, thus, does James Reeves use it?
What is, or should be, the prime function of the academic? Does
Reeves imply here that there is some confusion about this
amongst the committee men?

The French Master

How does Dannie Abse enable one to enter into his memories of the changes in Walter Wazo's temperament as if one were experiencing these changes just as the pupils did in the classroom? To what extent is Abse concerned with presenting Walter Wazo as a study of the type of teacher whom one loved to hate and whose temporary mellowing of character merely invoked derision of a different kind? Is Dannie Abse concerned to underline the gratuitous cruelty of boys to a vulnerable master as being something he is only *now* aware of? Does he, apart from the final line, indicate any signs of regret for the boys' feelings about Walter Wazo? Alternatively, does the recreating of Wazo's appearance and habits on paper also recreate the old feelings as intensely as ever for the writer and is this reflected in the style of the poem and in various evocative words and phrases such as 'sneaky' and 'tweaked'?

'Here Comes Sir George'

Dannie Abse's attitude to Walter Wazo may be equivocal, but Jon Stallworthy's motives for writing about 'Sir George' quickly become clear. What precisely are these motives? What similarities perhaps exist between Sir George's and Walter Wazo's pupils? What is Jon Stallworthy's view of the boys' reactions to Sir George? In what ways was Sir George's experience of life greatly different from that of Walter Wazo, and how is this reflected in the personal details given of both characters? What suggestions are there that their schools may also have been very different in environment?

In a poem entitled 'Letter to A Friend', Jon Stallworthy claims that,

> ...my poems all
> Are woven out of love's loose ends,
> For myself and for my friends.

What signs are there of Jon Stallworthy's writing 'Here Comes Sir George' as a poem 'woven out of love's loose ends'?

A Letter from a Lady in London

Dear Alice, you'll laugh when you know it, –
    Last week, at the Duchess's ball,
I danced with the clever new poet,
    You've heard of him, – Tully St Paul.
Miss Jonquil was perfectly frantic;
    I wish you had seen Lady Anne!
It really was very romantic;
    He *is* such a talented man!

He came up from Brazennose College,
    'Just caught', as they call it, last Spring;
And his head, love, is stuffed full of knowledge
    Of every conceivable thing:
Of science and logic he chatters,
    As fine and as fast as he can;
Though *I* am no judge of such matters,
    I'm sure he's a talented man.

His stories and jests are delightful; –
    Not stories or jests, dear, for *you*; –
The jests are exceedingly spiteful,
    The stories not always *quite* true.
Perhaps to be kind and veracious
    May do pretty well at Lausanne;
But it never would answer, – good gracious!
    Chez nous, in a talented man.

He sneers, – how my Alice would scold him! –
    At the bliss of a sigh or a tear;
He laughed, – only think, – when I told him
    How we cried o'er Trevelyan[1] last year.
I vow I was quite in a passion;
    I broke all the sticks of my fan;
But sentiment's quite out of fashion,
    It seems, in a talented man.

Lady Bab, who is terribly moral,
    Declared that poor Tully is vain,
And apt, – which is silly, – to quarrel,
    And fond, – which is wrong – of Champagne.
I listened and doubted, dear Alice;
    For I saw, when my Lady began,
It was only the Dowager's malice;
        She *does* hate a talented man!

He's hideous, – I own it. – But fame, love,
    Is all that these eyes can adore:
He's lame; – but Lord Byron was lame, love,
    And dumpy; – but so is Tom Moore.[2]
Then his voice, – *such* a voice! my sweet creature,
    It's like your Aunt Lucy's Toucan;
But oh! what's a tone or a feature,
    When once one's a talented man?

My mother, you know, all the season,
    Has talked of Sir Geoffrey's estate;
And truly, to do the fool reason,
    He *has* been less horrid of late.
But today, when we drive in the carriage,
    I'll tell her to lay down her plan; –
If ever I venture on marriage,
    It *must* be a talented man!

                Dora

P.S. – I have found, on reflection,
    One fault in my friend, – *entre nous*; –
Without it he'd just be perfection; –
    Poor fellow, – he has not a *sou*.
And so, when he comes in September
    To shoot with my Uncle, Sir Dan,
I've promised Mamma to remember
    He's *only* a talented man!

                Winthrop Mackworth Praed

[1] the title of a new novel by Caroline Lucy, Lady Scott, published in 1831
[2] for an example of Tom Moore's poetry see page 57

Winthrop Mackworth Redivivus

It's for Regency now I'm enthusing
    So we've Regency stripes on the wall
And – my dear, really frightf'lly amusing –
    A dome of wax fruit in the hall.
We've put the Van Gogh in the bathroom,
    Those sunflowers looked *so* out of date,
But instead, as there's plenty of hearth room,
    Real ivy grows out of the grate.

And plants for indoors are the fashion –
    Or so the *News Chronicle* said –
So I've ventured some housekeeping cash on
    A cactus which seems to be dead.
An artist with whom we're acquainted
    Has stippled the dining-room stove
And the walls are alternately painted
    Off-yellow and festival mauve.

The Minister's made the decision
    That Cedric's department must stay
So an O.B.E. (Civil Division)
    Will shortly be coming his way.
To you, dear, and also to me, dear,
    It's nothing, for you are a friend,
Not even if you and I see, dear,
    A knighthood, perhaps, in the end.

But it wasn't for this that I fill'd a
    Whole page up with gossip of course.
No: I'm dreadf'lly concerned for Matilda,
    Who seems to believe she's a horse.
She neighs when we're sitting at table
    And clutches a make-believe rein.
Her playroom she fancies a stable.
    Do you think she is going insane?

I know I would not let them christen her –
    Such an old superstition's absurd –
But when Cedric was reading *The Listener*
    Before he tuned in to the Third,
She walked on all fours like a dumb thing
    And nibbled my plants, I'm afraid.
Do you think we could exorcize something
    If we called in the Church to our aid?

Ex-horse-ize – that's rather funny –
    But it's not very funny to me
For I've spent all her grandmother's money
    On analysis since she was three.
And just when we'd freed her libido
    We went off to Venice and Rome
(You'll remember we met on the Lido)
    And left dear Matilda at home.

I'm afraid that that Riding School did it,
    The one where we sent her to stay;
Were she horse-mad before, then she hid it
    Or her analyst kept it at bay.
But that capable woman in Surrey
    Who seemed so reliable too,
Said 'Leave her to me and don't worry,
    This place is as good as the Zoo.

When she's not on a horse she's not idle;
    She can muck out the stables and clean
Her snaffle and saddle and bridle
    Till bed-time at seven-fifteen.'
Twenty guineas a week was the price, dear,
    For Matilda it may have been bliss,
But for us it is not very nice, dear,
    To find it has left her like this.

John Betjeman

NOTES

A Letter from a Lady in London

This poem dates from the early 1830s. Winthrop Mackworth Praed (1802–39) was a barrister and MP as well as being a writer of light verse. Why is the verse letter such an appropriate medium for a poem designed for social comment or for light-hearted send-ups of social behaviour? What techniques of construction does the poet use here to make the letter read convincingly as a letter and how do these techniques help to reveal Dora's character and social attitudes? How, in this poem, does the regular rhythm and the regular rhyming scheme contribute to the comedy? What is the overall effect of ending each verse with the phrase 'a talented man' and why is this a key phrase in the poem? Light verse can be very revealing of the age for and in which it was written. What does the poem appear to reflect of the social attitudes of upper class society in the England of the 1830s?

Winthrop Mackworth Redivivus

What does the title of the poem suggest about John Betjeman's intentions in writing it? Why does Betjeman's construction and style so accurately echo that of Winthrop Mackworth Praed? What, in this poem, is revealed of the character and social attitudes of the imaginary writer? What does the poem appear to reflect of the social attitudes of upper middle class society in the 1950s, when it was written? What is the tone of this poem? Is it critical, or tolerant, or something of both?

The poetry of social comment tends to date somewhat because of its obvious tendency to be concerned with conditions topical at the time of writing. What topical elements in both poems have naturally dated? What elements in both poems enable them to be enjoyed still, notwithstanding the topical references?

Splendid Girls

Those splendid girls at the wheels of powerful cars,
Sheer mechanism setting off slender charms.
I glimpse daredevil smiles as they whip past.

What are they all eager for, driving so fast
That I see them only momentarily? They are
Wholly desirable for half a heart-beat.

They have such style, such red nails! They are so neat!
But though they appear to drive at a dangerous speed
They do not do anything at random, that's for sure.

So keep your shirt on, they are spoken for.
They are as bright and lively as advertisements
For cigarettes or petrol or soap.

But there is no danger, and there is no hope.
Those reckless smiles have been carefully painted.
They are that sort of doll.

Everything, but everything, is under control.

John Normanton

Seascape

Always those beautiful girls;
Figureheads at the prow,
Taking a turn at the helm,
Coiling a rope at the stern;
Slim against the skyline
In Neptune-seducing slacks.
Where do they all come from?
The cabin-cruiser itself –
Twenty-thousand pounds if a penny –
That's easy enough,
Simply a question of money.
But the girls?

Ah, yes.
I expect you're right.

Stanley Sharpless

NOTES

Splendid Girls

What male illusions about 'those splendid girls at the wheels of powerful cars' are dispelled by this poem? Why is the poem dotted with words such as 'powerful', 'daredevil', 'eager', 'dangerous' and 'reckless', and what is the significance of the final phrase 'under control'? Why does John Normanton write of the girls being 'as bright and lively as advertisements for cigarettes or petrol or soap'? What does this poem seem to imply about such advertisements, and does it suggest that the poem carries with it some sort of social comment on the ways in which the use of sex symbols in advertising can condition male attitudes towards *any* 'splendid girl' seen driving a powerful car? Do you get the impression that the *writer* has been conditioned?

Seascape

What similarities exist, do you think, between the details of *this* poem and those in the poem 'Splendid Girls'? In what ways, however, are the emphases very different? How, perhaps, is this reflected in the endings of both poems? What is the effect of the studied avoidance of a direct answer to his question at the end of Stanley Sharpless's poem, and how does this reflect the overall tone of the poem? What effect is created by the short yet leisured lines of this poem in contrast to the longer, brasher lines of 'Splendid Girls'?

He Fell Among Thieves

'Ye have robbed,' said he, 'ye have slaughtered and made an end,
 Take your ill-got plunder, and bury the dead:
What will ye more of your guest and sometime friend?'
 'Blood for our blood,' they said.

He laugh'd: 'If one may settle the score for five,
 I am ready: but let the reckoning stand till day:
I have loved the sunlight as dearly as any alive.'
 'You shall die at dawn,' said they.

He flung his empty revolver down the slope,
 He climb'd alone to the Eastward edge of the trees;
All night long in a dream untroubled of hope
 He brooded, clasping his knees.

He did not hear the monotonous roar that fills
 The ravine where the Yassin river sullenly flows;
He did not see the starlight on the Laspur hills,
 Or the far Afghan snows.

He saw the April noon on his books aglow,
 The wistaria trailing in at the window wide;
He heard his father's voice from the terrace below
 Calling him down to ride.

He saw the gray little church across the park,
 The mounds that hide the loved and honoured dead;
The Norman arch, the chancel softly dark,
 The brasses black and red.

He saw the School Close, sunny and green,
 The runner beside him, the stand by the parapet wall,
The distant tape, and the crowd roaring between
 His own name over all.

He saw the dark wainscot and timbered roof,
 The long tables, and the faces merry and keen,
The College Eight and their trainer dining aloof,
 The Dons on the dais serene.

He watch'd the liner's stem ploughing the foam,
    He felt her trembling speed and the thrash of her screw;
He heard the passengers' voices talking of home,
    He saw the flag she flew.

And now it was dawn. He rose strong on his feet,
    And strode to his ruin'd camp below the wood;
He drank the breath of the morning cool and sweet;
    His murderers round him stood.

Light on the Laspur hills was broadening fast,
    The blood-red snow-peaks chilled to a dazzling white;
He turn'd, and saw the golden circle at last,
    Cut by the Eastern height.

'O glorious Life, Who dwellest in earth and sun,
I have lived, I praise and adore thee.'
                    A sword swept.
Over the pass the voices one by one
    Faded, and the hill slept.

Sir Henry Newbolt

Imperialists in Retirement

'I have done the State some service . . .' – Othello

Tender each to the other, gentle
But not to the world which has just now
Snatched back its gifts. Oh fallen, fallen
From your proconsular state! I watch
Perhaps too closely, with too much
Easy pity, the old man's loving
Protective gesture – the old woman
Accepting the arm of a blind man,
Leaning upon it. I look around
At the faded chintz, at china chipped
By so many packings, unpackings.

I listen, too. This part is not so
Easy. He is not resigned. He cries
Aloud for the state he kept. He wants
Privilege still, and power – the long

Moonlit nights of the steamship voyage
Out to a new appointment. Whisky
And bridge and talk of what's to be done –
The phrase again: 'They're children really.'
And he beats with feeble hands against
The immovable door of blindness,
The shut door of the years. 'Live in the
Past,' he says. 'That's the thing. Live in the
Past.' And his wife soothes him, as one would
A child when it's nearly his bedtime.
'One mustn't grumble,' she says. 'Times change.'

Her hands are reddened and swollen I
Notice, saying goodnight. Her head shakes.
She stumbles a little in rising.
Tonight she washes up. Tomorrow
She will scrub their kitchen on her knees.
I see, as we go, the look of love
From her to him blind. Then the door shuts.

Edward Lucie-Smith

NOTES

He Fell Among Thieves

The poetry of Sir Henry Newbolt, immensely popular during the earlier decades of the twentieth century when the large areas of red on the world map symbolised the might of the British Empire, has become less fashionable now that imperialism has become, to many, an emotively hostile word.

'He Fell Among Thieves' needs to be considered in the context of the original commitment of Newbolt to write a poem which reflected the assumption of many in his time that a privileged home, and a public school and Oxbridge education, produced the colonial army officers and administrators who were the backbone of the Empire. Whether or not one accepts the social implications, this assumption was then correct, and 'He Fell Among Thieves' presents the archetypal portrait of the young man whose pedigree allows him to die unflinchingly on the Indian frontier.

141

With these qualifications, one might then consider the skill with which Newbolt constructs this poem to achieve the maximum evocative effect for the readers *of his time*. What is his intention in placing the verbs describing the hero's actions in places of emphasis – 'He laughed . . . he flung . . . he did not hear . . . he saw . . . he rose . . . he drank . . . he turned'? How does his selection of details and his choice of descriptive words in the 'flash-back' verse help to underline the sense of the hero's present bravery and stoicism being conditioned by his past environment? By what means does he heighten the drama of the death sentence and its final execution?

Taking this poem as an example, what would you consider to be the qualities of Newbolt's writing which made a great appeal to a very large section of the British public for many years?

Imperialists in Retirement

What range of definition does the word 'imperialist' possess in the title of this poem?

In what ways is it clear that Edward Lucie-Smith is viewing the role of the imperialist from the standpoint of a much later generation than that of Newbolt? (Edward Lucie-Smith was born in 1933.) How does he underline the irony of retirement and ageing for a character whose working life has been one of 'privilege' and 'power'? What special irony now exists in the attitude of the 'imperialist' in the poem towards the natives of the country he was administering? What aspects of the poem reveal that Edward Lucie-Smith is concerned with the pathos of the old man's present condition and with the registering of muted disapproval of what remains of the original *public* figure? To what extent might the original intention to write this poem have been motivated by the poet's obvious sympathy for the wife and the role she has to play? What does he reveal of this role and of its special problems when a woman is married to a public figure whose position implies for her a subsidiary public role yet an increasingly vital private role as her husband ages?

The Burial of Sir John Moore at Corunna

Not a drum was heard, not a funeral note,
    As his corpse to the rampart we hurried;
Not a soldier discharged his farewell shot
    O'er the grave where our hero we buried.

We buried him darkly at dead of night,
    The sods with our bayonets turning;
By the struggling moonbeam's misty light
    And the lantern dimly burning.

No useless coffin enclosed his breast,
    Not in sheet or in shroud we wound him;
But he lay like a warrior taking his rest,
    With his martial cloak around him.

Few and short were the prayers we said,
    And we spoke not a word of sorrow;
But we steadfastly gazed on the face that was dead,
    And we bitterly thought of the morrow.

We thought, as we hollow'd his narrow bed
    And smoothed down his lonely pillow,
That the foe and the stranger would tread o'er his head,
    And we far away on the billow!

Lightly they'll talk of the spirit that's gone
    And o'er his cold ashes upbraid him, –
But little he'll reck, if they let him sleep on
    In the grave where a Briton has laid him.

But half of our heavy task was done
    When the clock struck the hour for retiring:
And we heard the distant and random gun
    That the foe was sullenly firing.

Slowly and sadly we laid him down,
    From the field of his fame fresh and gory;
We carved not a line, and we raised not a stone –
    But we left him alone with his glory.

Charles Wolfe

First World War Generals

These are of a different sort,
hugely-moustached, big-boned,
untransformable by art,
with heads and necks of blunt stone.

Legs tightly and smoothly gaitered,
impervious to an impudent wound,
Imagine these generals' good-natured
enormous jokes, rolled around.

Nor was the awkward dangling sword
unceremoniously stained
by doubting blood that slowly stirred
under the forehead, thickly veined.

If others imperishably scattered
wear poppies under foreign wind
and by the grass and glory uttered
seduce by death this stubborn land:

the deathless generals are gathered
like blocks of granite in the mind
for where those others change and glitter
these will not yield an inch of ground.

Iain Crichton Smith

The General

'Good-morning; good-morning!' the General said
When we met him last week on our way to the line.
Now the soldiers he smiled at are most of 'em dead,
And we're cursing his staff for incompetent swine.
'He's a cheery old card,' grunted Harry to Jack
As they slogged up to Arras with rifle and pack.

But he did for them both by his plan of attack.

Siegfried Sassoon

NOTES

The Burial of Sir John Moore at Corunna

Sir John Moore commanded the British troops during the first stage of the campaign in the Spanish Peninsula against the forces of Napoleon. His enterprising military strategy and personal bravery impressed Englishmen at home, and his death in battle at Corunna was regarded as a major tragedy. (After his death, command of the British forces was assumed by the Duke of Wellington.)

These were the days of personal command by generals actively involved in the fighting, and the poem by Charles Wolfe (1791–1823) records Sir John Moore's burial on the field of battle.

Why was it necessary for the burial of this great leader to be performed without the necessary ceremonial, do you think? Although the burial was hasty, the poet is able to convey the sense of dignity which nevertheless prevailed. How does he achieve this? Look particularly at the metre and the rhythms and emphases created in, for instance, the memorable line:

Slowly and sadly we laid him down.

To what extent does the setting of this poem in the form of an eye-witness account enhance its total effect as an elegaic poem?

First World War Generals

Like the Duke of Plaza Toro who, in Gilbert and Sullivan's comic opera *The Gondoliers*, 'led his regiment from behind when there was any fighting', some of the Generals of the First World War whose strategies produced the huge casualties in battles such as the Somme were not conspicuous for their personal leadership in the actual field of battle. Hostility towards them has grown with the years.

Commenting on General Haig's remark at the time of the German Offensive of April 1918 ('With our backs to the wall and believing in the justice of our own cause each one of us must fight to the end'), the historian A. J. P. Taylor observed in his book *English History 1914–1945* (1965):

In England this sentence was ranked with Nelson's last message. At the front, the prospect of Staff Officers fighting with their backs to the walls of their luxurious chateaux had less effect.

Iain Crichton Smith's poem is taken from a collection also published relatively recently, in 1961. What impression of the Generals does he create by his reference to 'heads and necks of blunt stone' and to their being 'gathered like blocks of granite in the mind'? Is this reference to their being 'untransformable by art' concerned with the difficulty of creating an artistic view of them – whether in a portrait photograph, a painting, or a poem? What evidence does his poem reveal of the capacity of those who actually died *in battle* to become transformed into what might be termed an 'imperishable' life through the medium of creative art? (To test this idea read through 'The Burial of Sir John Moore at Corunna' again or, better, look at some of the front-line poems of Wilfred Owen and his contemporaries.)

The General

What are your reactions to this revealing poem by Siegfried Sassoon, himself a front-line infantry officer during the First World War? How does its style and the terse economy of its detail underline the bitterness and disillusionment of those who had to implement the strategies of the Generals?

Three Barrows Down

In those fields haunted by fear
And a memory of soldiers –
Where the white road curves
From the blackened mill
By Ileden and Womenswold
Towards the tree-capped hill –

There in those summer-gold
And wide-flung pastures
The ear is cozened still
By the bare and empty song
Of evil forgotten days
And echo of ancient wrong;

And walking in the old ways
By the high banks and hedges
I come again to the dark
Three-barrowed wood and hear
In the summer-haunted stillness
That litany of fear;

And like a subtle illness
Invading blood and tissue,
From fields far and near
Creeps the rank smell of fighting,
The infection of the squaddies'
Bare-limbed and red-faced hating:

Whose muscled, belted bodies
Straddle the ditch and hedgeside
With rawboned violence, waiting
For the dark, predestined hour –
The harsh and bitter seeding.
Of the dragon-rooted flower.

Their eyes unheeding
Of storm-dark horizon,
And white-capped water-tower
Pricking the sullen line
Of the wood whose trees conceal
Tombs of an older time.

O betony and self-heal
Be near to salve the wounds
Of warrior and rookie
In the embattled hour:
And give to the queer and lonely
The brief and phallic power

To conquer and be only
Unkind to the swing-fed bloke
And pious white-faced sergeant
Who in the vernal hour
With evil would revoke
The dawn, the springing flower.

Jocelyn Brooke

The Drill-Sergeant

Shaped what was given him (shaped, in this case, us)
Made bellies flat and spines more rigorous,
Changed ways of walking, overhauled the brain's
Response to voices. Bilious epicure,
He tasted belts and rifles, shaves and shines.
I hear him at it, baying on the square.

His blasphemies are matters of technique,
Chisels and hammers. I am cross-grained teak,
Most obdurately awkward of the squad;
I blunt his edges, shoulder back his blows
(Though he can't strike me, blows are understood).
With no pride to be broken, I break his.

For now, presenting arms, I feel my rifle
Jump, almost, from my grasp; I hear him stifle
Under that lip so fiercely plumed with hair
An impatient sigh. That sudden gust of breath
Puffing the mottled cheeks, puffs down the dire
Image of all drill-sergeants, kills the myth.

Edward Lucie-Smith

148

Arthur McBride

I once knew a fellow named Arthur McBride,
And he and I rambled down by the sea-side,
A-looking for pleasure or what might betide,
And the weather was pleasant and charming.

So gaily and gallant we went on our tramp,
And we met Sergeant Harper and Corporal Cramp,
And the little wee fellow who roused up the camp
With his row-de-dow-dow in the morning.

'Good morning, young fellows,' the sergeant he cried.
'And the same to you, sergeant,' was all our reply.
There was nothing more spoken; we made to pass by
And continue our walk in the morning.

'Well now, my fine fellows, if you will enlist,
A guinea in gold I will slap in your fist,
And a crown in the bargain to kick up the dust
And drink the Queen's health in the morning.'

'Oh, no, mister sergeant, we aren't for sale.
We'll make no such bargain, and your bribe won't avail.
We're not tired of our country, and don't care to sail,
Though your offer is pleasant and charming.

If we were such fools as to take your advance,
It's right b * * * y slender would be our poor chance,
For the Queen wouldn't scruple to send us to France
And get us all shot in the morning.'

'Ha now, you young blackguards, if you say one more word,
I swear by the herrins, I'll draw out my sword
And run through your bodies as my strength may afford;
So now, you young b * * * s, take warning!'

Well, we beat that bold drummer as flat as a shoe,
And we make a football of his row-de-dow-do,
And as for the others, we knocked out the two.
Oh, we were the boys in that morning!

We took the old weapons that hung by their side
And flung them as far as we could in the tide.
'May the devil go with you,' says Arthur McBride,
'For delaying our walk this fine morning!'

Anon

NOTES

Three Barrows Down

Conscription for military service during the Second World War brought writers and poets into another world of army camps, a raw male-dominated existence centred initially around basic infantry training. Many camps were located in the countryside of Southern England (Womenswold is in Kent), and the routines of army life often seemed strangely at odds with the rural surroundings of the camps – a contrast outlined in Henry Reed's pair of poems, 'Judging Distance' and 'Naming of Parts'.

Few inmates of army camps in the open landscapes of southern England would be likely to notice, as Jocelyn Brooke did, the frequent close proximity of the camps to the barrow cemeteries which abound, for instance, in Wiltshire and Dorset. A writer once described parts of these two counties as 'the land of the living dead' because of the profusion of these ancient and evocative memorials of pre-Roman times. The title of this poem illustrates the way in which the presence of barrows is often indicated in local place names: 'Three Barrows Down'. Unexcavated barrows especially create a disturbing sense of presence and a sense of historical continuity, of a thread reaching back to one's primitive ancestors. How are these senses heightened by Jocelyn Brooke in this poem? In what ways does he establish links between past and present which emphasise his contact as a *new* soldier ('squaddies' and 'rookies' are terms given to new soldiers in training) with recurring forces of violence and evil?

'Betony' is a plant formerly credited with medicinal and magical properties. What is the special purpose of Jocelyn Brooke's invocation here? Why does he use the 'pious white-faced sergeant' as a symbol of the quality of evil which denies creativity – 'the dawn, the springing flower'?

The isolated situation of many camps necessitated the building of water-towers to supply them, and these water-towers became incongruous landmarks in the landscapes.

The phrase 'swing-fed' may refer to a soldier whose musical interests were confined to 'swing' – a popular, watered-down form of jazz much enjoyed during the late 1930s and the early 1940s.

The Drill-Sergeant

To the conscripted soldier who experienced the Second World War, or to the National Serviceman afterwards, the most dislikeable public figure was often the Drill-Sergeant, an artist whose art was perfected only by his total insensitivity and by his ability to fashion men into obedient automata. In what ways does this poem reveal this ability of the Drill-Sergeant to fashion his men? Why is it essential to Edward Lucie-Smith to expose the imperfections of this particular artist, and how is the imperfection revealed? Why is it necessary for him to use the word 'myth'? What does the Drill-Sergeant perhaps possess in common with Jocelyn Brooke's 'pious white-faced sergeant' in 'Three Barrows Down', and in what ways might the two poets share some common thoughts on the 'mythical' role of sergeants?

Arthur McBride

In the eighteenth and nineteenth centuries, one of the most intimidating figures for young men in both rural and industrial areas was that of the recruiting sergeant who, if not as notoriously violent as the press-gangs that sought unwilling recruits for the navy, was certainly renowned for the deception involved in persuading a man to accept the King or Queen's Shilling, a symbolic and binding act of agreement to serve in the Army.

'Arthur McBride' is of unknown authorship and, like many folk-songs of national social protest, it was performed throughout Britain. Versions of such songs varied from area to area. This version was actually recorded for the BBC early in 1939 by a singer from Walberswick, Suffolk.

Compared with, for example, Edward Lucie-Smith's 'The Drill-Sergeant', in what ways does this poem reveal that it was written to be sung, and in what ways does it suggest that it was composed with a popular, unsophisticated audience in mind, probably by an unsophisticated writer? What is the special appeal of songs of this nature to such an audience? Why is the use of conversation an effective feature of narrative poems and songs?

Elements of social protest exist in all three of these poems about soldiers. In what ways do the elements of protest in the poems by Jocelyn Brooke and Edward Lucie-Smith differ radically from the element of protest in 'Arthur McBride'?

My Master and I

Says the master to me, is it true? I am told
Your name on the books of the Union's enroll'd,
I can never allow that a workman of mine
With wicked disturbers of peace should combine.

Says I to the master, it's perfectly true
That I am in the Union, and I'll stick to it too,
And if between Union and you I must choose
I have plenty to win and little to lose.

For twenty years mostly my bread has been dry,
And to butter it now I shall certainly try;
And tho' I respect you, remember I'm free,
No master in England shall trample on me.

Says the master to me, a word or two more,
We never have quarrelled on matters before,
If you stick to the Union, ere long I'll be bound,
You will come and ask me for more wages all round.

Now I cannot afford more than two bob a day
When I look at the taxes and rent that I pay,
And the crops are so injured by game as you see,
If it is hard for you it's hard also for me.

Says I to the master I do not see how
Any need has arisen for quarrelling now,
And tho' likely enough we shall ask for more wage
I can promise you we shall not get first in a rage.

Anon

A New Song on the Turn-Out

Hurra for every sporting blade,
Of Liverpool and Birkenhead,
That will support the strike in trade,
    Against the Master Builders;
Let every man now well agree,
United in society,
The banners of sweet liberty,
    Will crown your cause most glorious.
        Hurrah, &c.

The master men are not content,
Unless that you will give consent,
To sign a binding document,
    Against the law of nature.
Why should you rob your family,
And drive yourselves to misery,
To yield unto their tyranny,
    Of silly Master Builders.

In order for to put you down,
The masters went to London town,
To get assistance from the crown,
    They spoke to Sir James Graham.
Their journey it was all in vain,
Altho' they went upon the train,
They're turning light all in the brain,
    The strike will soon be ended.

You bricklayers and you masons all,
You Carpenters both great and small,
Be firm and do not shrink at all,
    Unto the Master Builders;
The Master Builders in a squad,
Will dance to the tune of Moll-in-the-Wad,
The gallant men that carry the hod,
    Does cry out no surrender.

See Scotland's sons, as brave as Bruce,
As wild as tigers when let loose,
Does cry against the great abuse,
    Of silly Master Builders;
For while one penny's in the funds,
And boxes will be over-runn'd,
The Master Builders will be stunned
    To see the trades in union.

That silly elf they call S. H * * * s,
Will shortly have to go break stones,
Or else go gather rags and bones,
    For toffy in the morning.
His buildings are going to decay,
Before the 21st of May,
Unto the strike he must give way,
    Like men be well united.

Now Mr T * * * n how do you do,
I am none the better of seeing you,
You've got me in a pretty stew,
    My buildings are all idle,
I have much reason for to fret,
I never will be out of debt,
The strike I never will forget,
    You silly Sammy sly boots.

So to conclude and make an end,
Success attend each loyal friend,
That will a hand to freedom lend,
    To crush Monopoly;
Be firm, undaunted, loyal and true,
The Master Builders you'll subdue,
They are beginning to look blue,
    The tyrannizing creatures.

Anon
McCall, printer,
81, Cheapside, Liverpool

The Blackleg Miners

Oh, early in the evenin', just after dark,
The blackleg miners creep te wark,
Wi' their moleskin trousers an' dorty short,
There go the blackleg miners!

They take their picks an' doon they go
Te dig the coal that lies belaw,
An there's not a woman in this toon-raw[1]
Will look at a blackleg miner.

Oh, Delaval is a terrible place.
They rub wet clay in a blackleg's face,
An' roond the pit-heaps they run a foot-race
Wi' the dorty blackleg miners.

Now, don't go near the Seghill mine.
Across the way they stretch a line,
Te catch the throat an' break the spine
O' the dorty blackleg miners.

154

They'll take your tools an' duds as well,
An' hoy them doon the pit o' hell.
It's doon ye go, an' fare ye well,
Ye dorty blackleg miners!

So join the union while ye may.
Don't wait till your dyin' day,
For that may not be far away,
Ye dorty blackleg miners!

Anon

[1] town-row

NOTES

My Master and I

This Victorian street ballad should be considered in the context of
the poverty of rural labourers during the nineteenth century and
the attempts to form trade unions to represent the labourers. In
1834 a group of agricultural labourers from Dorset were tried and
sentenced to transportation for seven years for administering 'un-
lawful oaths' at their union initiation ceremonies. The labourers
became known as 'The Tolpuddle Martyrs' after the name of the
Dorset village a few miles to the east of Dorchester. Later, in 1870,
Joseph Arch, from Warwickshire, was a key figure in the organisa-
tion of Agricultural Labourers' Unions and in the mounting of
pressures to improve working and living conditions for the labourers.

How does the tone of this ballad – relatively conciliatory, one
might feel – suggest that membership of an agricultural union involved a more cautious and sensitive approach to the rural
labourer's master than that required by the factory worker in
urban areas? What fear is the labourer in this ballad most concerned to allay in his master? What is apt in the style of this
ballad, bearing in mind the people to whom it was directed?

A New Song on the Turn-Out

This is an example of a locally produced broadsheet prepared for sale in the streets and directed at a very local industrial dispute. The 'Turn-Out' occurred in 1846 when master builders in Liverpool and Birkenhead, feeling 'compelled to federate for mutual protection against the aggressive and unreasonable demands of the building trade', founded the Liverpool Master Builders Association and tried to press their workers into signing a binding employment contract. In this broadsheet 'S. H * * * s' was the Association's first President, Mr S. Holmes, and 'Mr. T * * * n' was probably a Mr W. Tomkinson of William Tomkinson and Sons.

What differences of attitude do you find between the writers of this broadsheet and the ballad 'My Master and I'? In what ways is 'A New Song on the Turn-Out' delightfully immoderate in tone? Why is this, do you think? Does its style reflect a greater confidence and aggressive power in nineteenth century urban labour as compared with rural labour, and if so why should this be? To what extent is the impudence of the broadsheet motivated by the fact that the building trade, on account of its craft element, might well possess greater bargaining power when unionised than would nineteenth century *factory* workers in dispute? What would be the general purpose of the publication of a broadsheet of this nature?

Note: a lithographic reproduction of the original of this and many other Liverpool street songs and broadside ballads can be found in *Liverpool Packets No. 1*, published by Scouse Press, 4 Windermere Terrace, Liverpool 8.

The Blackleg Miners

The mid-nineteenth century witnessed some bitter and highly justifiable strikes of miners against the individual pit-owners, strikes made the more bitter by owners' proposals actually to cut wages when coal prices fell, by the turning out of miners' families from their homes by the pit-owners during the strikes, and by the employment of blackleg miners.

This ballad, written for singing, originated in Durham, where there was a major strike in the mines in 1844. What differences in tone and style do you find between this ballad and 'A New Song on the Turn-Out', and what are the economic reasons for the differences, do you think? In what ways is both style and verse form well suited to reflect the thoughts and the tone of *this* ballad?

The Smokeless Chimney

by a Lancashire Lady (E. J. B.)[1]

Traveller on the Northern Railway!
　　Look and learn, as on you speed;
See the hundred smokeless chimneys;
　　Learn their tale of cheerless need.

'How much prettier is this county!'
　　Says the careless passer-by;
'Clouds of smoke we see no longer,
　　What's the reason? – tell me why.

'Better far it were, most surely,
　　Never more such clouds to see,
Bringing taint o'er nature's beauty,
　　With their foul obscurity.'

Thoughtless fair one! from yon chimney
　　Floats the golden breath of life;
Stop that current at your pleasure!
　　Stop! and starve the child – the wife.

Ah! to them each smokeless chimney
　　Is a signal of despair;
They see hunger, sickness, ruin,
　　Written in that pure, bright air.

'Mother! mother! see! 'twas truly
　　Said last week the mill would stop;
Mark yon chimney, nought is going,
　　There's no smoke from out o' th' top!

'Father! father! what's the reason
　　That the chimneys smokeless stand?
Is it true that all through strangers,
　　We must starve in our own land?'

Low upon her chair that mother
　　Droops, and sighs with tearful eye;
At the hearthstone lags the father,
　　Musing o'er the days gone by.

Days which saw him glad and hearty,
    Punctual at his work of love;
When the week's end brought him plenty,
    And he thank'd the Lord above.

When his wages, earn'd so justly,
    Gave him clothing, home, and food;
When his wife, with fond caresses,
    Bless'd his heart, so kind and good.

Neat and clean each Sunday saw them,
    In their place of prayer and praise,
Little dreaming that the morrow
    Piteous cries for help would raise.

Weeks roll on, and still yon chimney
    Gives of better times no sign;
Men by thousands cry for labour,
    Daily cry, and daily pine.

Now the things, so long and dearly
    Prized before, are pledged away;
Clock and Bible, marriage presents,
    Both must go – how sad to say!

Charley trots to school no longer,
    Nelly grows more pale each day;
Nay, the baby's shoes, so tiny,
    Must be sold, for bread to pay.

They who loathe to be dependent,
    Now for alms are forced to ask;
Hard is mill-work, but believe me,
    Begging is the bitterest task.

Soon will come the doom most dreaded,
    With a horror that appals;
Lo! before their downcast faces
    Grimly stare the workhouse walls.

Stranger, if these sorrows touch you,
    Widely bid your bounty flow;
And assist my poor endeavours
    To relieve this load of woe.

Let no more the smokeless chimneys
    Draw from you one word of praise;
Think, oh, think upon the thousands
    Who are moaning out their days.

Rather pray that, peace soon bringing
    Work and plenty in her train,
We may see these smokeless chimneys
    Blackening all the land again.

[1] See the note for this poem (page 163).

The Collier Lass

My name's Polly Parker, I come o'er from Worsley.
My father and mother work in the coal mine.
Our family's large, we have got seven children,
So I am obliged to work in the same mine.
    And as this is my fortune, I know you feel sorry
    That in such employment my days I shall pass,
    But I keep up my spirits, I sing and look merry
    Although I am but a poor collier lass.

By the greatest of dangers each day I'm surrounded.
I hang in the air by a rope or a chain.
The mine may fall in, I may be killed or wounded,
May perish by damp or the fire of the train.
    And what would you do if it were not for our labour?
    In wretched starvation your days you would pass,
    While we could provide you with life's greatest blessing.
    Then do not despise the poor collier lass.

All the day long you may say we are buried,
Deprived of the light and the warmth of the sun.
And often at nights from our bed we are hurried;
The water is in, and barefoot we run.
    And though we go ragged and black are our faces,
    As kind and as free as the best we'll be found,
    And our hearts are as white as your lords in fine places,
    Although we're poor colliers that work underground.

I am growing up fast, somehow or other.
There's a collier lad strangely runs in my mind.
And in spite of the talking of father and mother,
I think I should marry if he was inclined.
>   But should he prove surly and will not befriend me,
>   Another and better chance may come to pass;
>   And my friends here I know, to him will recommend me,
>   And I'll be no longer a collier lass.

Anon
Printed by Harkness of Preston

Poverty Knock

Poverty, poverty knock!
Me loom is a-sayin' all day.
Poverty, poverty knock!
Gaffer's too skinny to pay.
Poverty, poverty knock!
Keepin' one eye on the clock.
Ah know ah can guttle[1]
When ah hear me shuttle
Go: Poverty, poverty knock!

Up every mornin' at five.
Ah wonder that we keep alive.
Tired an' yawnin' on the cold mornin',
It's back to the dreary old drive.

Oh dear, we're goin' to be late.
Gaffer is stood at the gate.
We're out o' pocket, our wages they're docket;
We'll 'a' to buy grub on the slate.

An' when our wages they'll bring,
We're often short of a string.[2]
While we are fratchin'[3] wi' gaffer for snatchin',
We know to his brass he will cling.

We've got to wet our own yarn
By dippin' it into the tarn.
It's wet an' soggy an' makes us feel groggy,
An' there's mice in that dirty old barn.

Oh dear, me poor 'ead it sings.
Ah should have woven three strings,
But threads are breakin' and my back is achin'.
Oh dear, ah wish ah had wings.

Sometimes a shuttle flies out,
Give some poor woman a clout.
Ther she lies bleedin', but nobody's 'eedin'.
Who's goin' t'carry her out?

Tuner[4] should tackle me loom.
'E'd rather sit on his bum.
'E's far too busy a-courtin' our Lizzie,
An' ah cannat get 'im to come.

Lizzie is so easy led.
All think that 'e teks her to bed.
She allus was skinny, now look at her pinny.
It's just about time they was wed.

Poverty, poverty knock!
Me loom is a-sayin' all day.
Poverty, poverty knock!
Gaffer's too skinny to pay.
Poverty, poverty knock!
Keepin' one eye on the clock.
Ah know ah can guttle
When ah hear me shuttle
Go: Poverty, poverty knock!

Anon

[1] eat
[2] length of cloth
[3] quarrelling
[4] loom-maintenance man

The Song of the Lower Classes

We plough and sow – we're so very, very low,
    That we delve in the dirty clay,
Till we bless the plain – with the golden grain,
    And the vale with the fragrant hay,

Our place we know, – we're so very low,
    'Tis down at the landlord's feet:
We're not too low – the bread to grow,
    But too low the bread to eat.

Down, down we go, – we're so very low,
    To the hell of the deep sunk mines,
But we gather the proudest gems that glow,
    When the crown of a despot shines.
And whenever he lacks – upon our backs
    Fresh loads he deigns to lay:
We're far too low to vote the tax,
    But not too low to pay.

We're low – we're low – mere rabble, we know
    But, at our plastic power,
The mould at the lordling's feet will grow
    Into palace and church and tower.
Then prostrate fall – in the rich man's hall,
    And cringe at the rich man's door;
We're not too low to build the wall,
    But too low to tread the floor.

We're low – we're low – we're very very low,
    Yet from our fingers glide
The silken flow – and the robes that glow
    Round the limbs of the sons of pride.
And what we get – and what we give –
    We know, and we know our share;
We're not too low the cloth to weave,
    But too low the Cloth to wear!

We're low – we're low – we're very very low,
    And yet when the trumpets ring,
The thrust of a poor man's arm will go
    Thro' the heart of the proudest King.
We're low – we're low – our place we know,
    We're only the rank and file,
We're not too low – to kill the foe,
    But too low to touch the spoil.

Ernest Jones

NOTES

The Smokeless Chimney

Drawing attention to the poverty and distress created by the growth of the factory system and of attendant industrial towns from the late eighteenth century onwards was a process not by any means confined to the writers of popular industrial songs and broadsheets. Middle class novelists such as Charles Dickens and Mrs Gaskell were notable for their concern. The Victorian politician and novelist, Benjamin Disraeli, shocked his readers with his portrayal of working class poverty in his novel *Sybil* – subtitled 'The Two Nations', a reference to the separate states of poverty and affluence in Victorian England. In Parliament some of the most vital reforms of working conditions in industrial areas were achieved through the efforts of the aristocrat Lord Ashley, Seventh Earl of Shaftesbury.

This poem provides a modest example of the operation of social conscience on the part of 'a lady' prepared to use her ability to compose competent verse to help raise money for a relief fund. The 'lady' came from the Lancashire 'minor gentry'; she was the daughter of William Garnett, Esq., of Quernmore Park and Bleasdale, near Lancaster. Her verses were printed on a card and were sold mainly at principal railway stations in North West England. Their sales realised £160 for the Relief Fund, a considerable amount then.

How does the writer set about directing her appeal to the traveller in particular? In what ways does the emphasis on the smokeless chimneys make possible a link between the hoped-for sympathy and charity of the travellers and the feelings of the unemployed? Which details in the poem are obviously included to stir both conscience and pity in the readers? Bearing in mind that this poem is also a direct appeal for money, which emotive words and phrases are obviously used with some deliberation? What suggestions are there in the presentation of ideas in the poem and in the style of the poem that the writer's commitments are sincere and are not assumed for the purpose of the poem?

If one possessed no information about the writer other than the evidence of the poem itself, how could you tell that it was written by an educated person conversant with the formal techniques of poetic composition rather than by one of the unsophisticated broadsheet writers of the time?

The Collier Lass

In the early 1840s England was shocked by the publication of the First Report of the Children's Employment Commission. It revealed that children of seven and eight years of age were employed in most coal mines and that some mines employed even younger children. Even more disturbing was the fact that girls as well as boys worked in the mines, frequently crawling along low passages dragging burdens to which they were attached by chains. The Report led to the passing of the Coal Mines Act which forbade the employment of women and children underground. This ballad was printed by Harkness of Preston, Lancashire, well-known printers of broadsheet ballads, at about the time that the Commission was receiving evidence from women employed in the mines, and it clearly presented an accurate picture of conditions. It is thus an interesting example of one of the growing number of protest songs circulating in the industrial areas of England during the mid-nineteenth century. In what ways does the mode of presentation of this ballad and the selection of details underline its intention to stir the consciences of those who read or hear it? What is 'Polly Parker' anxious to establish about her character and her role in society?

Poverty Knock

The cotton mills of Lancashire and the woollen mills of Yorkshire, like the coal mines, made extensive use of the labour of women and children during the nineteenth century. The health of women working in the factories was often ruined by the long hours of standing at work in the hot, humid, and crowded mills.

The practice of singing whilst spinning and weaving went back to the days of domestic industry and it was continued in the textile mills, often in the form of hymns, many Methodists being employed in the mills. This song, an authentic work song, the refrain of which was inspired by the sound made by the Dobbie loom, an early mechanical loom used for plain weaving ('Po-ver-ty-knock'), might have been lost but for a recording made by A. G. Green in 1965 of its being sung by an old weaver, Tom Daniel, from Batley in Yorkshire. Daniel had learnt the song at the mill where he worked on leaving school early in this century. He explained to Mr Green that the reference in the song to the fact that the injured woman's workmates did not go to help her when she was hit by the flying shuttle emphasises that the weavers could not afford to stop to help because they were on piece-work – i.e. paid in terms of the amount they produced.

How does the rhythm of the song and the use of internal rhymes help to emphasise the pressures under which the weavers worked and the overall feelings both of the monotony of their working day and the insecurity of their positions? In what ways does the style, the use of dialect, and the occasional flash of humour help to bring the listener (or the reader) into intimate contact with the world of the Yorkshire weaver in the nineteenth century?

You can find the music for 'Poverty Knock' in A. L. Lloyd's very interesting book *Folk Song in England*, published in 1967 by Lawrence and Wishart Ltd.

The Song of the Lower Classes

Between 1838 and 1848 a group of individuals made three unsuccessful attempts to present to Parliament their policy document, the 'People's Charter', which demanded, amongst other things, universal male suffrage and vote by ballot. Their Charter led to supporters of their movement being known as Chartists, and although their political hopes were unrealised, the Chartists did much, through their well-supported meetings and processions in the industrial towns and cities of Britain, to arouse social conscience regarding the condition of the rural and urban poor and the absence of a working-class voice in the affairs of the nation.

Ernest Jones (1819–69), the writer of this ballad, was one of the leaders of the Chartist Movement and a prolific writer and versifier. What is the real purpose of his verse by verse references to various working activities of the lower classes? What evidence is there that he is concerned in the ballad with political protest and with class distinctions rather than with the actual *conditions* of poverty? In what ways does the use of language in this poem suggest (as did that of 'A Lady' in 'The Smokeless Chimney') that Ernest Jones is accustomed to writing poetry rather than vernacular ballads? Do you get the impression that Ernest Jones really feels for the human condition of the lower classes or is he more concerned with projecting a Chartist image? How does his sense of personal involvement seem to compare with that of 'A Lancashire Lady' in 'The Smokeless Chimney'?

The Murder of Maria Marten by W. Corder

Come all you thoughtless young men, a warning take by me,
And think upon my unhappy fate to be hanged upon a tree;
My name is William Corder, to you I do declare,
I courted Maria Marten, most beautiful and fair.

I promised I would marry her upon a certain day,
Instead of that, I was resolved to take her life away.
I went into her father's house the 18th day of May,
Saying, my dear Maria, we will fix the wedding day.

If you will meet me at the Red-barn, as sure as I have life,
I will take you to Ipswich town, and there make you my wife;
I then went home and fetched my gun, my pickaxe and my spade,
I went into the Red-barn, and there I dug her grave.

With heart so light, she thought no harm, to meet him she did go,
He murdered her all in the barn, and laid her body low:
After the horrible deed was done, she lay weltering in her gore,
Her bleeding mangled body he buried beneath the Red-barn floor.

Now all things being silent, her spirit could not rest,
She appeared unto her mother, who suckled her at her breast;
For many a long month or more, her mind being sore oppress'd,
Neither night or day she could not take any rest.

Her mother's mind being so disturbed, she dreamt three nights
       o'er,
Her daughter she lay murdered beneath the Red-barn floor;
She sent the father to the barn, when he the ground did thrust,
And there he found his daughter mingling with the dust.

My trial is hard, I could not stand, most woeful was the sight,
When her jaw-bone was brought to prove, which pierced my heart
       quite;
Her aged father standing by, likewise his loving wife,
And in her grief her hair she tore, she scarcely could keep life.

Adieu, adieu, my loving friends, my glass is almost run,
On Monday next will be my last, when I am to be hang'd;
So you, young men, who do pass by, with pity look on me,
For murdering Maria Marten, I was hang'd upon the tree.

James Catnach

The Terrible Destruction of the Liverpool Landing Stage

Kind friends now around me your attention I call,
For the cause of my verses has upset us all;
We are rather cut up in this go-a-head age,
All Liverpool grieves for the new Landing Stage.

It will ne'er be forgotten in history's page,
The terrible fire on the new landing stage.

On Tuesday the 28th day of July,
Our New Landing Stage 'is on fire' was the cry;
We could not believe it, but when we got there,
The smoke in thick mountains was darkening the air.

All Liverpool then was struck with amaze,
And with feelings of pity upon it did gaze;
For in a short time to destruction was hurled,
The most magnificent Stage in the World.

The devouring flames they rose higher and higher,
And the Mersey's waves glittered and glowed with the fire.
The New Landing Stage like a furnace did gleam,
And burnt with a fury that never was seen.

The strong iron girders when burnt in the fire,
Were twisted as easy as small bits of wire;
The fruits of hard work and the engineers brains
Was quickly destroyed by the work of the flames.

The poor Cheshire people looked most awful black,
They came o'er the ferries but could not get back;
And one cranky Welshman got nearly smoke-dried,
Looking out for the steamer for Birkenhead side.

There was all sorts of people stood at the fire,
Some to dislike, and some to admire;
Some found a sweetheart in ladies so bold,
Some lost their money and some found a cold.

May the Stage stand for ever when erected again,
And never no more be devoured by the flame;
Tho' the opening can't be when the Queen's son is here,
He'll come down on purpose you need never fear.

It will ne'er be forgotten in history's page,
The terrible fire on the new landing stage.

Anon

The Tay Bridge Disaster

Beautiful Railway Bridge of the Silv'ry Tay!
Alas! I am very sorry to say
That ninety lives have been taken away
On the last Sabbath day of 1879,
Which will be remember'd for a very long time.

'Twas about seven o'clock at night,
And the wind it blew with all its might,
And the rain came pouring down,
And the dark clouds seem'd to frown,
And the Demon of the air seem'd to say –
'I'll blow down the Bridge of Tay.'

When the train left Edinburgh
The passengers' hearts were light and felt no sorrow,
But Boreas blew a terrific gale,
Which made their hearts for to quail,
And many of the passengers with fear did say –
'I hope God will send us safe across the Bridge of Tay.'

But when the train came near to Wormit Bay,
Boreas he did loud and angry bray,
And shook the central girders of the Bridge of Tay
On the last Sabbath day of 1879,
Which will be remember'd for a very long time.

So the train sped on with all its might,
And Bonnie Dundee soon hove in sight,
And the passengers' hearts felt light,
Thinking they would enjoy themselves on the New Year,
With their friends at home they lov'd most dear,
And wish them all a happy New Year.

So the train mov'd slowly along the Bridge of Tay,
Until it was about midway,
Then the central girders with a crash gave way,
And down went the train and passengers into the Tay!
The Storm Fiend did loudly bray,
Because ninety lives had been taken away,
On the last Sabbath day of 1879,
Which will be remember'd for a very long time.

As soon as the catastrophe came to be known
The alarm from mouth to mouth was blown,
And the cry rang out all o'er the town,
Good Heavens! the Tay Bridge is blown down,
And a passenger train from Edinburgh,
Which fill'd all the people's hearts with sorrow,
And made them for to turn pale,
Because none of the passengers were sav'd to tell the tale
How the disaster happen'd on the last Sabbath day of 1879,
Which will be remember'd for a very long time.

It must have been an awful sight,
To witness in the dusky moonlight,
While the Storm Fiend did laugh, and angry did bray,
Along the Railway Bridge of the Silv'ry Tay.
Oh! ill-fated Bridge of the Silv'ry Tay,
I must now conclude my lay
By telling the world fearlessly without the least dismay,
That your central girders would not have given way,
At least many sensible men do say,
Had they been supported on each side with buttresses,
At least many sensible men confesses,
For the stronger we our houses do build,
The less chance we have of being killed.

William McGonagall

NOTES

The Murder of Maria Marten by W. Corder

An immensely popular form of broadsheet in the first half of the nineteenth century was that purporting to be the 'Last Dying Speech and Confession' of a notorious criminal, usually one who had committed a particularly nasty murder, before going to the gallows. Although such broadsheets were in the first instance topical publications, their popularity sometimes led to spin-offs which gave the stories a much longer currency. The account by James Catnach, a veteran broadsheet writer of accounts of murders and executions, of the 'Last Dying Speech and Confession' of W. Corder, murderer of Maria Marten, sold 1,166,000 copies. The story of the murder, 'the Red Barn Murder', near Ipswich in 1827, went on to become the subject of a play. The play in turn became one of the most frequently performed Victorian melodramas and it enjoys fairly regular revivals even today.

This poem forms the third part of a publication which included William Corder's alleged prose confession written in gaol at Bury St Edmunds in 1828, and a prose account of the execution itself.

Is there any special dramatic reason, do you think, for the writer's choosing to compose the fourth, fifth, and sixth verses in the *third* person ('he...she') rather than the first person ('I') of the rest of the poem? Look carefully at the details given in these three verses. How moral in intent ('a warning take by me') were these 'Confession' poems? What was probably their real purpose and how do the details of the poem and the style in which the details are presented seem to confirm this? For what type of reader and reader-interest would this poem perhaps be designed? (Remember that many people regarded watching an execution as an exciting outing then.) What makes the murder of Maria Marten one of the classic murder stories, do you think?

The Terrible Destruction of the Liverpool Landing Stage

The broadsheet writers catered for a public with an insatiable interest in murders, executions and disasters – particularly shipwrecks, fires, and tragedies involving spectacular loss of life. In this case, however, it was not loss of human life, but the destruction of an integral part of Liverpool seaboard life which prompted the lurid language of the broadsheet poet.

Before the building of the rail and road tunnels, journeys between Liverpool and the Wirral Peninsula of Cheshire and between Liverpool and North Wales involved the use of one of a number of ferries which plied continuously across the Mersey estuary at its narrowest point between Liverpool and Birkenhead. To cope with the wide tidal variations an elaborate 'floating' landing stage has long been a necessity for Liverpool if regular services are to maintained through the day. Because of the importance of the ferries, road transport has by tradition converged on Pier Head, overlooking the Landing Stage and the Mersey, and both the Landing Stage and the Pier Head have become legendary aspects of Liverpool life.

This poem records the destruction of George's Landing Stage on 28 July 1874 just before Queen Victoria's second son was due to visit Liverpool. A new landing stage was opened on 8 April 1876.

What aspects of the poem reveal that it was aimed essentially at local readers and that it appealed to local loyalties? In what ways is the versifier's lack of technique abundantly clear in the way he handles his material and in the significance (or otherwise!) of some of the details he includes? On the other hand, does the very amateurishness of the verse place the reader of today in closer proximity to the event described and to the reactions of the local populace to the event when it happened? (This broadsheet is reproduced in *Liverpool Packet No. 1*. See note on page 156.)

The Tay Bridge Disaster

William McGonagall, self-styled 'poet and tragedian' and Scotland's most famous 'bad' poet, wrote at least four poems featuring the Tay Bridge. He commemorated the opening of the first Tay Bridge on 12 May 1879 with his customary effusiveness and what turned out to be an ironic hope that God would 'protect all passengers by night and by day, and that no accident will befall them while crossing The Bridge of the Silvery Tay'. Little did he realise that his good wishes to the bridge's designer and engineer, Bouch, would soon be followed by the collapse of the bridge and by harsh criticisms of Bouch's faulty design and workmanship. McGonagall followed his commemorative poem with one on 'The Newport Railway' which extolled the advantages of the Bridge for housewives who could travel across it by train from Newport to Dundee to shop for 'cheap tea, bread, and jam, and also some of Lipton's ham'.

The first Tay Bridge collapsed during a severe gale at the end of December 1879, when a train was crossing the bridge, and after this disaster McGonagall quickly produced this poem.

Finally, when a new bridge was built, McGonagall was ready with 'An Address to the New Tay Bridge', praising its 'beautiful side-screens – which will be great protection on a windy day, so as the railway carriages won't be blown away...'

Had McGonagall not been so well known, first as an eccentric personality and later as a cult figure for those who were fascinated by the badness of his poetry, 'The Tay Bridge Disaster' might otherwise have merely taken its place as a good example of the popular type of nineteenth-century broadsheet poem dealing with dire disaster.

How does he manage to convey a sense of personality to this poem which is not to be found to the same extent in the anonymous poet's account of the destruction of the Liverpool Landing Stage on page 167?

McGonagall is the accidental master of ludicrous anticlimax – one can hardly call it bathos because the heights he descends from are rarely if ever elevated! How does he achieve these exquisite moments? What contribution is made by his use of rhyme and his use of poetic diction to what emerges as a distinctly personal style? Does irrelevancy of detail to the original intention of the poem and the sudden inclusion of prosaic observations – as in the last verse of this poem – also contribute to the uniqueness of McGonagall's creations?

Does the Tay Bridge disaster lose its terrible impact in this poem? If it does not, how does it avoid doing so; if it does, how is the loss of impact achieved?

'The Time I Discovered Myself to be a Poet'

The most startling incident in my life was the time I discovered myself to be a poet, which was in the year 1877. During the Dundee holiday week, in the bright and balmy month of June, when trees and flowers were in full bloom, while lonely and sad in my room, I sat thinking about the thousands of people who were away by rail and steamboat, perhaps to the land of Burns, or poor ill-treated Tannahill, or to gaze upon the Trossachs in Rob Roy's country, or elsewhere wherever their minds led them. Well, while pondering so, I seemed to feel as it were a strange kind of feeling stealing over me, and remained so for about five minutes. A flame, as Lord Byron has said, seemed to kindle up my entire frame, along with a strong desire to write poetry; and I felt so happy, so happy, that I was inclined to dance, then I began to pace backwards and forwards in the room, trying to shake off all thought of writing poetry; but the more I tried, the more strong the sensation became. It was so strong, I imagined that a pen was in my right hand, and a voice crying, 'Write Write!' So I said to myself, ruminating, let me see; what shall I write? then all at once a bright idea struck me to write about my best friend, the late Reverend George Gilfillan; in my opinion I could not have chosen a better subject, therefore I immediately found paper, pen, and ink, and set myself down to immortalize the great preacher, poet, and orator. These are the lines I penned, which I dropped into the box of the *Weekly News* office surreptitiously, which appeared in that paper as follows: –

'W. M'G., Dundee, who modestly seeks to hide his light under a bushel, has surreptitiously dropped into our letter-box an address to the Rev. George Gilfillan. Here is a sample of this worthy's powers of versification: –

'Rev. George Gilfillan of Dundee,
    There is none can you excel;
You have boldly rejected the Confession of Faith,
    And defended your cause right well.

'The first time I heard him speak
    'Twas in the Kinnaird Hall,
Lecturing on the Garibaldi movement,
    As loud as he could bawl.

'He is a liberal gentleman
To the poor while in distress,
And for his kindness unto them
    The Lord will surely bless.

'My blessing on his noble form,
    And on his lofty head,
May all good angels guard him while living,
    And hereafter when he's dead.'

P.S. – This is the first poem that I composed while under the
divine inspiration, and is true, as I have to give an account to God
at the day of judgement for all the sins I have committed.

William McGonagall

(from his *Brief Autobiography*)

Stillborn

These poems do not live: it's a sad diagnosis.
They grew their toes and fingers well enough,
Their little foreheads bulged with concentration.
If they missed out on walking about like people
It wasn't for any lack of mother-love.

O I cannot understand what happened to them!
They are proper in shape and number and every part.
They sit so nicely in the pickling fluid!
They smile and smile and smile and smile at me.
And still the lungs won't fill and the heart won't start.

They are not pigs, they are not even fish,
Though they have a piggy and a fishy air –
It would be better if they were alive, and that's what they were.
But they are dead, and their mother near dead with distraction,
And they stupidly stare, and do not speak of her.

Sylvia Plath

Trees

They were talking about trees in the office,
and I was sneaking a look at an anthology of poetry,
and I came across this poem in which someone asked
if the poet had written a tree poem. It was a good
question, and I thought about it myself. I'd written
a couple of poems which mentioned trees, and one
in which a lady lived in a tree, and there was another
poem which said that you can't talk to trees.
You can talk to people, or at least some of them,
but not to trees. I mean, who'd want to lie in bed
next to a tree and try to make conversation afterwards?
It's bad enough with certain women, but a tree!
And it would probably be Autumn and the bloody thing
would be shedding its leaves all over the sheets,
and that's even worse than a woman who sheds tears.
So, I thought, no, I hadn't ever written a proper tree
poem, and I was pretty sure I never would, then I
had another look at the poem in the anthology, and
I realised the poet wasn't writing about trees,
not really. When I listened in to the conversation
in the office, they weren't really talking about trees,
either, but outside the window the tall, slim trees
were gracefully swaying in the wind, and I started
watching them closely, and thinking that loving
a tree might not be too bad a thing, after all.
I wasn't really thinking about trees, of course.

Jim Burns

Sonnet

Nuns fret not at their convent's narrow room;
And hermits are contented with their cells;
And students with their pensive citadels;
Maids at the wheel, the weaver at his loom,
Sit blithe and happy; bees that soar for bloom,
High as the highest Peak of Furness-fells,
Will murmur by the hour in foxglove bells:
In truth, the prison, unto which we doom
Ourselves, no prison is: and hence for me,
In sundry moods, 'twas pastime to be bound
Within the Sonnet's scanty plot of ground;
Pleased if some Souls (for such there needs must be)
Who have felt the weight of too much liberty,
Should find brief solace there, as I have found.

William Wordsworth

Sonnet: On First Looking into Chapman's Homer

Much have I travelled in the realms of gold,
   And many goodly states and kingdoms seen;
   Round many western islands have I been
Which bards in fealty to Apollo hold.
Oft of one wide expanse had I been told
   That deep-browed Homer ruled as his demesne;
   Yet did I never breathe its pure serene
Till I heard Chapman speak out loud and bold:
Then felt I like some watcher of the skies
   When a new planet swims into his ken;
Or like stout Cortez when with eagle eyes
   He stared at the Pacific – and all his men
Looked at each other with a wild surmise –
   Silent, upon a peak in Darien.

John Keats

NOTES

'The Time I Discovered Myself to be a Poet'

This extract from William McGonagall's *Brief Autobiography* reveals something of the naïve self-confidence in his creative ability which enabled him to produce a large and widely-read body of bad poetry. What probably enables his verse to be so outrageously entertaining is that he sincerely felt himself to have been inspired and to be a poet, and this sincerity of belief enabled him to write oblivious of appalling rhymes, repetition of details and an assemblage of quite incredibly trivial supporting description and banal comment. Even so, his poetry possesses some unmistakably individual qualities, including a style which both admirers and detractors have enjoyed imitating.

What aspects of 'The Tay Bridge Disaster' (p. 168) – and the lines on Gilfillan – possess the inimitable McGonagall touch?

Do you think that writing 'poetry' came easily to McGonagall? What makes his concept of the process of poetic inspiration, as revealed in this extract, so naïve?

Stillborn

In Virginia Woolf's novel *To The Lighthouse*, Lily Briscoe is concerned with the completion of a painting:

> She could see it all so clearly, so commandingly, when she looked: it was when she took her brush in hand that the whole thing changed. It was in that moment's flight between the picture and her canvas that the demons set on her who often brought her to the verge of tears and made this passage from conception to work as dreadful as any down a dark passage for a child.

Both Virginia Woolf and Sylvia Plath were subject to enormous mental tensions in the creation of their writings; both writers were able from hard experience to describe these tensions; both committed suicide.

How does Sylvia Plath use the imagery of physical stillbirth to give a precise view of the processes involved in the production of what she considers to be a poetic failure, and how do these images clarify the reader's understanding of the trauma of producing a poem which the writer has to acknowledge as a failure? How is the sense of the mental disturbance which affects the writer at the time conveyed in the poem? How does Sylvia Plath suggest that the act of completing the poems so that they exist on the page in print makes the experience of failure the greater?

Trees

Why is this poem a much more valid exploration of the true qualities of poetry and the writing of poetry than that made by McGonagall in his *Brief Autobiography* (p. 173)?

In what ways does this poem seem to present a comic view of the writing of the kind of poetry which uses aspects of nature as symbols for aspects of human life? How does Jim Burns make use of an informally conversational style, first to give an impression of casual, light-hearted chat and then to reveal that the chat contains a great deal of sensitive, valid thought about reading, interpreting and writing poetry which uses symbols? How serious is Jim Burns's poem? How do you view it here when it is placed alongside Sylvia Plath's painful account of the agonies of creating a poem? Why can some poetry be relatively easy to write whilst other poetry is distressingly difficult? Is it a question of subject, or level, or inspiration, or of personal standards of creative and poetic discipline?

Sonnet: Nuns Fret Not at Their Convent's Narrow Room

Discuss the interactions in this sonnet through which Wordsworth illustrates not only the satisfactions which can be gained from lives lived within closely limited bounds but also the satisfactions which the poet can gain from confining his inspiration within the fourteen lines of the sonnet. How do these interactions in fact illustrate the rich creative potential available 'within the Sonnet's scanty plot of ground'? Why is the image depicting the sonnet as a 'scanty plot of ground' so apt and so unifying in the circumstances?

What are the special creative disciplines involved in the use of the sonnet form? Why might poets 'find brief solace there' and why does Wordsworth see in freer poetic forms 'the weight of too much liberty'?

Does this poem complement Sylvia Plath's 'Stillborn' in any way by throwing additional light on the difficulties of writing poetry? Might the freer forms of modern verse such as that used by Sylvia Plath in her poem place greater strain on the more sensitive contemporary writers than those imposed on poets using the more organised formal structures of traditional poetry in the past, with their precise uses of rhyme and metre?

Sonnet: On First Looking into Chapman's Homer

Lord Houghton (Richard Monckton Milnes, 1809–85) in his book, *Life and Letters of John Keats*, recalls the circumstances which inspired this Sonnet:

> Unable as he [Keats] was to read the original Greek, Homer had as yet been to him a name of solemn significance, and nothing more. His friend and literary counsellor, Mr Clarke, happened to borrow Chapman's translation, and having invited Keats to read it with him one evening, they continued their study till daylight. He describes Keats's delight as intense, even to shouting aloud, as some passage of especial energy struck his imagination... The Sonnet in which these his first impressions are concentrated, was left the following day on Mr Clarke's table...

Discuss the ways in which Keats's images of travel and discovery – particularly in the last six lines – demonstrate the richness of experience which can be contained within 'the Sonnet's scanty plot of ground'. Bearing in mind especially the last four lines of this sonnet, what makes it so much more than a celebration of one man's excitement after reading one book in 1816? Try to define why this poem might possess an appeal which *cannot* be diminished by the passage of time.

Index of first lines

Acknowledgements

We are grateful to the following for permission to reproduce copyright material:

The author's agents for Dannie Abse's poems 'The Magician' and 'The French Master' from *Collected Poems* published by Hutchinson 1977; the author's agents on behalf of the estate of the late Jocelyn Brooke for the poem 'Three Barrows Down' by Jocelyn Brooke in *December Spring*; Martin Secker & Warburg Ltd and the author, Alan Brownjohn for the poem 'Vital' from *A Song of Good Life*; the author, Heather Buck for the poem 'Moving House' *PEN New Poems 1976–77* published by Hutchinson; John Calder (Publishers) Ltd for an extract from the poem 'Stravinsky' by Robert Siohau, translated by Eric Walter White; Jonathan Cape Ltd on behalf of the estate of William Plomer for his poems 'At a Memorial Service' and 'The Axe in the Orchard' from *Celebrations* and 'Caledonian Market' from *Collected Poems*; Jonathan Cape Ltd on behalf of the executors of the W. H. Davies Estate for the poem 'My Old Acquaintance' from *The Complete Poems of W. H. Davies*; Jonathan Cape Ltd on behalf of the executors of the estate of C. Day Lewis and Hogarth Press for the poems 'You that love England . . .' from *The Magnetic Mountain* and 'Watching Post' from *Collected Poems 1954* by C. Day Lewis; Carcanet Press Ltd and the author, Andrew Waterman for his poem 'An Ulster Garland' published in *From the Other Country*; the author, John Cassidy for his poem 'Summer' from *An Attitude of Mind* published by Hutchinson; the author's agents for Charles Causley's poems 'Reservoir Street' from *Underneath the Water* and 'The Ballad of Charlotte Dymond' from *Johnny Alleluia* published by Macmillan; Chatto and Windus Ltd for the poems 'A Small War' from *Mountains Polecats and Pheasants* by Leslie Norris 'Rome Remembered' from *Finding Gold* by Leslie Norris and 'Jodrell Bank' from *The World I See* by Patric Dickinson; the author, Iain Crichton-Smith for his poems 'At the Highland Games' and 'First World War Generals'; J. M. Dent & Sons Ltd for Clifford Dyment's poem 'The Dark City' from *Experience and Places*; Faber and Faber Ltd for the poems 'The Evacuees' from *Five Rivers* by Norman Nicholson, 'On the Move' from *The Sense of Movement* by Thom Gunn, 'The Suicide' from *The Collected Poems of Louis MacNeice*, 'Home is so Sad' from *The Whitsun Weddings* by Philip Larkin, 'Docker' from *Death of a Naturalist* by Seamus Heaney and 'The Unknown Citizen' from *Collected Shorter Poems* by W. H. Auden reprinted by permission of Faber and Faber Ltd; Victor Gollancz Ltd for the poem 'Nocturne' by Kingsley Amis in *A Case of Samples*; the author's agents and Robert Graves for his poems 'A Frosty Night' and 'Symptoms of Love' from *Collected Poems*; the author, Michael Hamburger and Carcanet Press for 'View from a Back Window' from *Real Estate*; William Heinemann Ltd for James Reeves's poems 'Primadonna' from *The Password*, 'An Academic' from *The Talking Skull* and 'Grand Opera' from *The Questioning Tiger*; the author, Alan Hill for his poem 'Belfast 1969' from *The Greentide* published by Rivelin Press; the author, Philip Hobsbaum for his poem 'Provincial Undergraduate' from *The Place's Fault and Other Poems* published by Macmillan 1964; Hogarth Press Ltd and the author's literary estate for an extract from *To the Lighthouse* by Virginia Woolf; Hogarth Press Ltd for 'Leader of Men' from *Surroundings* by Norman MacCraig; the poet, David Holbrook for his poem 'Poor Old Horse' © David Holbrook; Hutchinson General Books Ltd for 'Festival Notebook' from *Collected Poems 1979* by Kingsley Amis; the author's agents for Elizabeth Jenning's poems, 'Old Woman' from